THE MEMORY PLACE

HOW MY PARENTS SURVIVED NAZI HELL

MONICA VAN RIJN

ap

ISBN 9789493418561 (ebook)

ISBN 9789493418547 (paperback)

ISBN 9789493418554 (hardcover)

Publisher: Amsterdam Publishers, The Netherlands

info@amsterdampublishers.com

The Memory Place is part of the series *Holocaust Books for Young Adults*

This book was written entirely by the author, in the author's own words, without the use of generative AI or large language model tools.

CONTENTS

This book is dedicated to youngsters of all ages with little or no knowledge of World War II. We are all descendants of people who once fled from or survived a war. The scope of World War II is unprecedented and will remain a study subject for the largest ethnic cleansing crime committed on the human race. This is a true story, based on stories and facts relayed to me by my own family members. Names of most of the family and friends have been changed to protect the participants and their offspring.

PREFACE

When I was a little girl, I had sat in front of the bookcase of our Chicago apartment staring at the colorful collection of books before me. On the bottom shelf, all the way to the left, was one book with a rusty spiral binding that caught my eye. On the faded black cardboard front cover were two large white letters – SS – and above those in larger type was the title: *NAZI HELL*. At that time, however, I could not read nor write. It was not a large book, and it looked weathered and old. I was turning pages and stopped when I saw a photograph I could not understand. Pictured was a massive rectangular hole in the earth filled with naked bodies haphazardly tossed inside; one gigantic hole with countless corpses.

Just then, my mother appeared in the doorway and saw which book I was browsing through, panic quickly forming on her face. She screamed at me, ripped the book from my hands, and told me it was not a children's book. Her expression of horror did not escape me.

From that moment on, I kept asking her questions. Later, I discovered that she and my father had wanted to keep a very disturbing secret from my sister and me. At first, they avoided all questions about war by changing the subject. I would not let up, however, and kept asking. When I was a bit older, Mother did speak. My parents had both been persecuted in World War II for several years and had spent two years in captivity in 17 concentration camps, including two death camps. Each time my mother told me another inconceivable story of a concentration camp she or my father had been held captive in, and had survived, I was increasingly in awe of my parents. Even as a child I knew that my parents' incredible story needed to be told. I interviewed my mother throughout her life. Sometimes with pen and paper and sometimes on film. It was made very clear that my father was not available for questioning. Wanting to verify every story, I did extensive research on the internet and consulted the official websites of the major concentration camps; I found that my mother had an incredible memory for detail.

Until I was in my forties, the war did not play a huge part in our family. At least, not overtly. At first, I denied any interference in my life from my parents' World War II experiences. It happened to their generation, not to mine.

Later, as an adult, its devastating effects influenced not only my adult relationships, but I saw that it affected even the slightest decision I was in the process of making. That is also when certain themes began to emerge in my artwork. Art critics wrote about the traces of second-generation issues visible in my paintings. Themes related to Holocaust survivors, like "homecoming", "wandering", and "seeking refuge," were the themes that also seemed to fit my images. After several years of painting professionally, I did see a pattern develop in my work. Many years went by before I became aware of the way I depicted my need for security in my three-dimensional work. I invented an object I call an "art safe": it is a painting behind which lies a hidden compartment for securing items.

Later, I would find out why we came to America when I was an infant. By 1949, my parents had felt threatened in Europe once again. We were refugees fleeing from a threatening situation.

I did not know that I would be the one to write my parents' saga years later. I also could not know just how deeply their story would impact my own life. It took me more than 20 years to unravel everything and complete this manuscript.

The reader is taken along two paths, two timelines: one of my mother, Hetty, and one of my father, Fritz. Hetty is still a tortured captive of the German fascist Nazi regime in spring 1944. Fritz is traveling home as a free man one year later, in June 1945, after liberation. They have been separated for 14 months and neither of them know of each other's whereabouts or whether the other is dead or alive.

PART 1

WORLDS APART

1

HETTY, JUNE 3, 1944

ON TRANSPORT

Yesterday, the guards announced that the women prisoners were all going on transport by train; the news nearly made Hetty's illness relapse. She had just barely survived a bout with scarlet fever, one week before. Hetty and 400 women prisoners were being forced to leave the Dutch concentration camp, Vught, for a destination unknown. They had been incarcerated for precisely one year in a hostile, fenced-in, German-run Nazi prison camp in the southern part of the Netherlands. All the slave laborers worked 12-hour-long shifts, endured lengthy roll calls twice daily, and were barely fed. Even though the prisoners hated it there, they had at least come to know what to expect. Now there was complete upheaval in Hetty's mind.

The women had been alerted earlier that day to take cold showers and prepare for travel. They had no towels to dry off with. Afterward, all of the prisoners were issued flimsy, gray, formless uniforms to wear. Each one received a single outfit. They were forced to leave all possessions behind. Not even a toothbrush was allowed. Most of them had not had one since their arrival, when all of their possessions had been stolen from them. One of the German guards had entered the barracks and seemed to take perverse pleasure in his words: "Where you are going you won't need any possessions."

Now Hetty had one more thing to deal with: being in a constant state of fear, preparing for an unknown destination that was likely to be her last.

The German and Dutch Nazi guards were usually quite composed. Now they seemed to be in a hurry, committed to emptying the camp as fast as they could. They beat the prisoners with clubs and forced them to board a long freight train at three in the morning, with no explanation.

Hetty was furious over the guards' treatment. She and the others had always obeyed orders and done their work well, and now, even after being nearly starved to death, they were being clubbed and crammed into cattle cars as if they had misbehaved. Even the guards who knew them well seemed frantic and eager to be rid of them. The line of women prisoners was moving rapidly, but there was still a lengthy line to go; more than what this freight train could hold.

There were too many women for the space available in each cattle car. Most of the women were forced to stand, crammed together like sardines in a tin can. Hetty had to kneel if she had any hope of resting, let alone sleeping inside this overcrowded, filthy space. She had already become accustomed to the disgusting acrid odor of urine and feces coming from overflowing buckets that had to suffice as toilets.

Each person had been rationed one small hunk of bread called a *Kuch*. A *Kuch* was about the size of one-third of a loaf of bread. The guard said that it had to last for the entire trip. Yet, no one knew how long that might be; how long could that meager loaf last? They had not been given even a drop of drinking water, so Hetty thought the trip might be very short. The cattle car was dirty and dark, with no windows. The only minimal light, air, and contact with the outside world came from between narrow metal slats placed just below the roof for ventilation.

On the first day of this transport, the train stopped at a busy station in Nijmegen, near the Dutch-German border. It was the break of day and the beginning of rush hour. It turned out to be a long layover because there were empty cars being connected to their overcrowded ones. During this time, Hetty managed to borrow a tiny pencil from someone, then to find a scrap of paper. She scribbled an urgent message, dated it, addressed it, signed it, rolled it up, and climbing onto someone's shoulders, she tossed it from the car through the ventilation slats near the ceiling. She had no idea whether anyone outside even saw the paper fall, but she hoped with all her heart that someone might find it and deliver it to her dearest friends, the Van Dykes, in Amsterdam. It might be the last time anyone would hear from her. This could be her only chance to communicate with Olivia Van Dyke and her daughters, Fleur and Sally. She did not call out because she feared the consequences, so she silently prayed that her note would not vanish in the wind.

Concentration camp life in World War II was one of insecurity. Even though the daily routine was essentially unchanging, the strict adherence to the rules was torturous and demanding. The Nazis viewed their prisoners as subhuman, and this justified the use of violence. Shouted orders and dehumanizing remarks were used by all to belittle and weaken the morale of the detainees. This is how the established order within the camp was maintained. However, every day there could be unwanted, dreaded news. The immediate evacuation of the men back in March and now this evacuation of the women impacted them. "Why did we have to leave now? What did it mean? Was everyone being deported? Was the entire camp being evacuated? Where are we going to? These were the questions occupying Hetty's mind.

Hetty had first worked in a sewing studio in Camp Vught soon after her arrival one year ago. Those days were exhausting but stable. Once she had adjusted, she was aware that she was being useful. That is, until the men had been sent away. Her husband, Fritz Frankel, had vanished on that fateful day, March 20, 1944.

Camp Vught was a prison complex composed of many large factories hidden in the forest about an hour's walk from rows and rows of communal barracks. Men, women, and children were all living separately. Most families were split up, and family members could not communicate with one another. When the men were deported so suddenly, Escotex, the sewing studio Hetty worked in, was abruptly shut down.

Because Hetty and Fritz had both been schooled in the garment industry, they had been assigned to sew for Escotex, a formerly Jewish clothing manufacturer, now taken over by the Nazis. Hetty was an avid seamstress and a talented designer. She had hoped to someday establish herself as such, but when the war rumbled to life, that dream faded.

Her best day at Escotex was when Fritz had been appointed head of the sewing studio where she was already working. Before that, the only time they could see one another was at roll call. And only at a distance. During working hours, they saw each other daily. Fritz was an experienced fur designer and had been a supervisor of four departments in the De Klein clothing firm in Amsterdam. Because of his extensive experience and expertise, he was appointed to manage the workplace and do what he did best: oversee the making of the fur-lined flight jackets and coats needed for the German Wehrmacht, the Nazi air force, and the German war effort.

Many factories were set up inside the prison camp. The Nazis had taken over the production of certain products at the onset of the war which they needed for the war effort. Companies were forced to use these facilities, and the slave laborers had no freedoms. In this way the production would keep running smoothly and the Nazis had complete control.

All the new arrivals, including Hetty and Fritz, were distributed prison uniforms, with no attention paid to the size. The same disregard was shown when assigning wooden clogs. Some received two of the same foot. Every uniform had triangular patches of a certain color sewn onto their otherwise-identical outfits. Yellow was for Jews. The colored badges revealed the background of each prisoner and were an indication to the guards (and everyone else) of how they were going to be treated. Of the 25 categories, the Jews were to be given the harshest treatment. There was so much hatred toward the captives, especially the Jews. Neither Hetty nor Fritz had ever been treated this badly. Even though the camp was not originally planned as an extermination camp, there was a crematorium for the many who died from hunger, malnutrition, and abuse. They had all been deceived by the Nazis and were being held captive against their will.

The Philips Light Bulb factory in Eindhoven was, like Escotex, one of the companies with a factory inside the camp. Frederik Philips, the gentile director of the Philips company, had cut a deal with the Nazi commander at the head offices in Eindhoven in an attempt to protect his workers from going to work inside a camp. But, in spite of his efforts, most of the employees still ended up imprisoned. The director had only delayed the inevitable. Even so, he kept negotiating terms in an attempt to prevent their deportation to Eastern Europe, where he had heard death camps were located. Philips employed about 3,100 people, of whom 469 were Jewish. After the Escotex closure, Hetty and her small group were able to join the existing group of Philips workers. Philips had convinced the commanding authorities that it was imperative to use Jewish women with their long, slender fingers; otherwise, the long, narrow radio tubes so vital to the Nazi war effort could not be assembled correctly.

In fact, Philips had developed a special tube for exactly the purpose of defying and fooling the Nazis. These radio tubes were designed to disintegrate rapidly, thereby disabling the machinery that the Nazis had come to rely upon. He took a significant risk by doing this and would pay for this later on. The radio tubes were necessary for all kinds of equipment, for use in planes, ships, and submarines. Word was that Philips had negotiated an extra warm meal for his workers, which they called "the Philips Snack."

Hetty's group were now under the so-called employment, as slaves, of the Philips company, where they were afforded extra protection. In all, approximately 400 women and a few teenage girls became known as the "Philips group." Being one of them turned out to be good fortune for all the women, including Hetty.

Although she had cried for days after Fritz had been sent away, overcome with grief, her assignment to the Philips Group helped her regain her strength, and her mood lifted. Working on the conveyor belt making radios, Hetty was able to listen to an occasional BBC broadcast – something that was otherwise strictly forbidden. She eventually was able to get moved to a job working at the end of the assembly line, where the radios were tested. She would turn the dial on the radio as if she were testing it, but what she was really doing was searching for a news channel. She listened to the broadcasts she could find when no Nazis were around. Her ability to speak fluent German, English, and Dutch was an advantage. She made friends there with a German woman named Dottie, and they found it helpful knowing which of the guards did not understand Dutch.

The rude dismissal of the Philips Group and the knowledge that they were being deported gave Hetty and the others the impression that something dreadful was going to happen to them.

It felt like the enemy was getting nervous and had therefore sped up the deportations. Were the Nazis losing the war? The prisoners became even more despondent because, if the rumors were correct, deportation meant death. This is what Hetty had come to expect, since the guards kept terrorizing them with death threats. The Philips group of women were being sent away, and that was all they knew.

Hetty had heard that most of the prison trains leaving Camp Vught went straight to Auschwitz or another death camp in Poland. Any mention of extermination camps in the northeastern regions of Europe was meant to scare them and make them feel weak. Hetty knew Auschwitz was a notorious concentration camp in Poland. Scare her, it did. Yet, she could not really form a picture in her mind of what it would be like to be there.

After Nijmegen, the train stopped periodically, usually at smaller train stations. At each stop, she could hear German voices outside, usually shouting orders to others on the platforms, but no one answered any of her cries for help. *We must be in Germany, now,* she thought. She was getting further away from anything that resembled normal life. She knew she was getting even farther away from home. Hours turned into days. The bread had been gone by the end of that first day. There was no more food, and she saw no one. Although Hetty had never known such hunger, it was the thirst that nearly drove her mad. She was beside herself with craving for water. Thirst was so much worse than hunger. Others were sobbing in misery and pleading to unhearing Gods to be relieved of this nightmare.

The gusting winds and the nighttime temperatures caused goosebumps up and down her arms. But it was the unimaginable doom engulfing her that made her rub them for warmth and protection. Abandoned and alone among fellow inmates, she shivered. Hetty wondered whether her husband, Fritz, had also traveled these same rails when the Nazis had forced the men to leave

Camp Vught two-and-a-half months before. When the train crossed the border into Poland, the landscape changed again.

After three nights, Hetty awoke to a putrid scent that permeated everything. She could barely see anything in the dark space of the cattle car she was in. All she knew was that she and the others were at the mercy of cruel guards who were not responding. There had hardly been any communication amongst the other women once the shouting lessened, their tears dried up, and they became resigned to their fate.

There was no other choice but to stand on someone's shoulders if you wanted to get a glimpse of outside. Hetty climbed onto the shoulders of another woman prisoner to look through those air vents and report on what could be seen from the train. Her breath caught when she saw piles of bodies strewn over kilometers of fields in the distance. But it was the overwhelming toxic stench of burning flesh and sizzling hair reaching her nostrils that triggered a terror unlike anything she had known before. She covered her mouth and started to gag.

Hetty had to shout out above the rattling wheels of the train to describe what she was seeing. It was a menacing and desolate landscape of emptiness. In the distance, dozens of gray buildings stood behind at least five rows of high-voltage barbed wire fencing. Beyond that, in an area which appeared to be a city, high watchtowers studded the horizon for as far and wide as she could see. Her own worry was reflected in the eyes of the others. It seemed like they were approaching a death camp.

She recalled the last words a German guard at Camp Vught had uttered, just before the metal doors on the train cars had slammed shut: "Anyone leaving here by train will be going to one place and to one place only: to your own death. You are the walking dead now. *Auf Wiedersehen.*"

2

FRITZ, JUNE 3, 1945

RETURNING HOME

It had taken Fritz more than a month to get back to the German/Dutch border, still wearing his prison uniform. No one along the way had offered him a change of clothes. He dared not ask anyone for aid. He had received a small amount of money from the authorities who had freed him, but it was all gone now. After he had walked, traveled by train, and hitched a ride with a few other uniformed former prisoners, he was now entering Holland on the back of a flatbed truck. It was a curious scene: a small group of disheveled men returning home – all in prison garb with only a few meager belongings.

Fritz had a small bundle with him, containing a little food, a few rags, and an enamelware cup. That cup was his prized possession. For more than two years, he'd kept it firmly tied to his body because, without it, he would have received neither food nor water. Every prisoner was issued only one such cup. It was impossible for an onlooker to mistake any of them for anything but prisoners of war returning home.

Fritz was traveling back from Brünnlitz, Czechoslovakia, where he had been working in one of Oskar Schindler's factories. Schindler, a German Catholic industrialist, bought a formerly Jewish-owned enamelware factory, which he renamed "Emalia," and employed Jewish workers from the Krakow ghetto. At the beginning of the war, Schindler was an opportunist, cutting deals with the Nazis for profit, while also being a member of the Nazi party. As the war went on, however, Schindler slowly realized what was happening. He became aware of the dark, hidden agenda of the Nazi party to annihilate Jews from the face of the earth, and he became sympathetic to the Jews' suffering. Schindler was good to those who were interned in his factory, frequently intervening on their behalf with the Nazis. He also gave his workers certain liberties that were allowed nowhere else, such as allowing Jews to celebrate the sabbath in the barracks on Friday nights. It seemed, for many, extremely generous of him. Schindler was ultimately able to save the lives of 1,200 Jews working in his factories.

Now Fritz was alone with a few Dutch men on the last leg of his trip. All of them, just like Fritz, were anticipating a warm welcome upon homecoming.

However, no one approached them, helped them, or asked any questions along the way. Most seemed afraid of the men and their striped prison clothing. In any case, the Dutch were far too preoccupied with rebuilding their own lives. They, too, had suffered under the occupation of the Germans for the last five years.

Fritz had the eager, hopeful look of a survivor in his eyes. He had been imprisoned far away from anyone or anything that resembled normal life. He had spent the better part of two years in eight German and Polish concentration camps, under the worst conditions, where he was tortured and starved. He had also been imprisoned in the most infamous camp of them all: Auschwitz-Birkenau.

Auschwitz was a complex of over 40 camps created and run by the Nazis in occupied Poland. It operated for five years and was finally liberated by the Soviet Union on January 27, 1945. Fritz had survived even that. He was returning to Amsterdam on June 3, 1945, hoping to find somebody home. The war had lasted five years from the Dutch surrender on May 10, 1940, to the German surrender on May 5, 1945. The first three years of this war had been bad enough for Fritz, but the last two had been utterly devastating, unbearable, and inhumane, having been incarcerated for only one reason: having been born Jewish. Fritz had been mentally and physically brutalized. He had been held captive against his will and tortured by a hostile enemy. He was hoping to see a familiar and friendly face today, hoping to fall into someone's loving arms. But he did not know what he would find in this new Amsterdam.

As the truck slowly approached the city's edge, Fritz saw people walking around freely, smiling. It had been ages since he'd witnessed anything quite like that. The truck rolled along through familiar suburbs, passing rows of blossoming trees, and the apartment buildings where family members and friends had once lived. How many of his friends and colleagues might still be living there? The air seemed to hold the promise of picnics and relaxation, but not for Fritz. He was only concerned with finding his missing loved ones and wondering whether anyone still living in Amsterdam would welcome him or be sympathetic. Or if he would encounter more hostility, like he had frequently encountered during his journey home. Fritz wondered whether the aggression he had experienced in Polish concentration camps at the hands of Nazi soldiers would occur again in a post-war Holland.

Would the Dutch government and Royal family be helpful and empathetic to the plight of the enslaved Dutch citizens who had survived the war and were returning? Would they have their rights restored, and be able to find housing and jobs as before? Fritz had assumed they would but was not so sure. After all, the war had lasted only five days before the Dutch government capitulated. The Jews had not felt protected when the assault on their community had taken place, so why would Fritz expect more now?

The country had been overrun with Nazi soldiers who had beaten, berated, and abused anyone who wasn't blond and blue-eyed. The true hidden agenda of the Nazis was greater than the eradication of Jews. The real goal was to create a perfect race. Their hidden purpose had not been exposed until the second year of the war, when deportations to death camps were suspected. The Nazis targeted many minority groups that deviated from the light-skinned, tall, athletic features belonging to the Northern European and Scandinavian peoples, including the Dutch. The Nazis had already established breeding farms in various European countries to create an "Aryan" race. No one had seen this coming.

When the many millions of people who had been summoned to come willingly to train stations or Nazi headquarters were promised relocation for work, no one suspected anything like ethnic cleansing. There was an economic recession, after all. All kinds of citizens were offered new jobs at new locations in Germany, Poland, Czechoslovakia, and elsewhere. Dutch citizens had boarded trains heading East because they chose to believe what the Nazis had told them. They were promised good pay, housing, and communication with home. They would be free to move about, receive and send mail and packages from home, and continue their lives as usual. Until then, no one had believed any of the rumors suggesting otherwise. No one believed that they would relinquish their rights and lose their freedom. Who could have believed that the enemy had a strategy that intricate and sophisticated? Believing such rumors seemed unthinkable, and anyone spreading them must be conspiracy theorists because no one wanted to believe such evil. That death camps would have already been built for the purpose of the annihilation of certain minority groups, like the Jewish folk, was simply ludicrous.

The Dutch observed the returning prisoners, having no idea what to expect or to do about these emaciated-looking people with their deep-set-eyes. No one knew what the men on the truck had gone through – although by now, most of the Dutch had probably heard enough confirmation of the atrocities taking place in Eastern Europe to believe them.

Fritz had realized why people were reluctant to approach him. It was not because he was scary, but because they were afraid to get involved. How would these men react to intervention, advice, or even help? How would they ever be able to trust their own countrymen, knowing that about 25 percent of the Dutch citizens had collaborated with the enemy? Would those returning be welcome at home? Were the survivors no more than "damaged goods" who would never be capable of living in a civilized society again?

While traveling back, Fritz had heard on the news that many more camps than were initially thought to exist had been discovered. This news was shocking. More than shocking. Concentration camps were scattered throughout the entire European continent, North Africa, Indonesia, and Japan, and were divided into three categories: transit camps, work camps, and death camps. The Nazis had deliberately planned how the annihilation would occur. It would take years to establish an accurate count of all of them. All minority groups, including gays, gypsies, Jews, the disabled, and dark-skinned north African, Italian, Spanish, and Portuguese (all people whose coastal region was around the Mediterranean Sea were persecuted and massacred). There were 44,000 concentration camps in Europe and North Africa alone, and many of the liberators had said that they could be found by the smell.

The men riding on the flatbed truck had seen death intimately. They had been immersed in it. All had been tortured in more ways than starvation. All had had their dignity stripped from them. They had been robbed, separated from their families, and violated. Many of those along the roads where Fritz was traveling were watching them with uncomfortable expressions on their faces. Nobody had really expected them to return.

Had there ever been a more hateful, cruel war on this scale before? Fritz sat pondering. *There had been no crimes committed by any of us. We had been going about our daily routines of work, sleep, and play on that day our country was suddenly and without warning invaded.* These were Fritz's thoughts as he reminisced about how World War II had started in Warsaw, Poland, in 1939 with a surprise hostile takeover of a Polish radio station by a few disguised German Nazis. Now, they had access to the radio and started spreading vile fake news about how the attack had come to pass. They reported that Poland was the aggressor and had attacked Germany first, although that is not what happened. Germany falsely claimed they were retaliating, however, and war on Poland was declared.

During Fritz's journey back to his hometown, his hair had grown back somewhat; he had his mustache once again, and he had gained some weight. Physically, he was in good enough shape to travel. He was one of the fortunate ones. Many of the inmates he'd left behind in the concentration camps did not make it back at all. Even after the liberation of the camps by international allies, thousands of captives died of typhoid fever, hunger, or of the illnesses that ran rampant in the camps.

Fritz was at a crossroads now, commencing on a new and yet-to-be rebuilt life, hopefully in his home city of Amsterdam. He had first planned to go to Hetty's best friends, Olivia van Dyke and her two daughters at their home on the Amsteldijk.

However, he knew that, before he could ring their doorbell, he had better prepare himself for disappointment. Some scenarios were so frightening that he had refused to entertain them, until now. But he was determined to not let fear control him. He knew all too well what fear can do to a person. He also knew how it felt to rekindle hope.

He had pictured his arrival at the Van Dyke's residence innumerable times before; but now that he was approaching Amsterdam, he fought back the urge to weep. He didn't know whether this was due to relief at approaching his beloved city, or if it was just apprehension regarding the kind of reception he was about to experience at the end of this journey.

Would anybody he knew be at home? He truly hoped that somebody there would be able to tell him that his greatest love, his wife Hetty, was well and had also survived the war; yet Fritz knew that it would be nothing short of a miracle if she had. Knowing how close to death he himself had come on most days during the last two years of this terrible war, he could barely imagine how hard it would have been for someone as petite and giving as his wife Hetty to survive the brutality and strain of each predatory Nazi assault. He was determined that if she were alive somewhere, he would find her.

The image in his mind of Hetty Golden had on many days helped strengthen his will to live. Even now, her image was driving his determination to return to where their love and life together had begun. But, dead or alive, she still had a strong presence in his mind and heart. She had provided him with the courage and purpose to go on that he had needed many times during his captivity. The only question that mattered now was: *Where was she?*

When Fritz was liberated, he and all his fellow inmates were bald and skinny, including the women. The Nazis had lost the war, and most soldiers had abandoned their posts, on the run. The captives might have been free to go, yet they did not feel free. When all the Nazi guards fled, they had left the prisoners behind to die. Some inmates remained behind locked gates for days, and even though they survived the war, many still starved to death.

On his journey, he inquired as to Hetty's whereabouts at every city he stopped in or of people he met along the way. Unfortunately, no one had seen or heard anything about her. Fritz also read the headlines and found out how Europe was dealing with renewal and repair. All transportation had been paralyzed for months and was just starting up. He was hoping that the Netherlands, too, was on the mend. All he cared about now was finding Hetty.

Still, his longing for Hetty did not erase all the personal pain and torment he had experienced. Fritz was also aware of the possibility that the Van Dykes had been deported, too. If so, there would be nobody at home to return to. The fact that Fritz had been a witness to the destruction of an entire European way of life had him struggling with a deep, unrelenting sorrow that would haunt his dreams for the rest of his life.

Fritz Frankel, still in uniform, enroute to Amsterdam. These inmates traveled with him on the flatbed truck. The blackboard message in the background "THIS IS HOLLAND. REMEMBER! THE DUTCH ARE OUR ALLIES" indicates being at the Dutch border with Germany as well as that WWII has recently ended. Source: Col. de Booys, Gemeentearchief (Municipal Archives) Arnhem, the Netherlands; B1620-33/45

Hetty (from private collection)

3

HETTY, JUNE 1944

ALWAYS THE UNKNOWN

Hetty had last seen her husband, Fritz, two months ago, in March 1944. They had spent 10 months together in Camp Vught. They slept in separate barracks and could only view each other at a distance during roll calls in the large field where all the prisoners were assembled for that purpose. On the day he vanished, like every other day, all prisoners were forced to stand at attention for the head count. But on this particular day, no men were present. The women stood whispering to each other and asking whether anyone knew what had happened to the men. There had been no announcements and there had been no goodbyes. But later, when Hetty was walking back to the barracks, she spotted all the men in the distance, boarding trains. She saw a long line of male prisoners in striped uniforms lined up. That fateful morning, Hetty had been devastated.

Camp Vught had been built before Hetty and Fritz had arrived there. It was large and sprawling, like a small town, and was monitored by German surveillance equipment. Electrified barbed wire fencing and high watchtowers spaced at regular intervals surrounded the camp, making it impossible for Hetty to approach the trains where Fritz might be. Armed guards watched and patrolled everyone, at all times. It was off limits for prisoners to speak to the guards, and likewise, the guards were prohibited from conversing with the prisoners.

No one suspected that Hetty and Fritz were husband and wife, and they both wanted to keep it that way. If anyone in the sewing studio had known they were a couple, it could have made either of them more vulnerable. Most prisoners learned to keep secrets like that to themselves. It was the best protection. Just seeing Fritz every day at work had been Hetty's lifeline. They had found a way to communicate with one another: They would exchange tiny, rolled-up love notes and would enjoy the occasional furtive touch.

During their work in the Escotex sweatshop, despite the prohibition, Hetty and Fritz had nevertheless gotten to know a camp guard, whom they referred to as "Hunchy" (when he was out of earshot). He had a hunchback, and, although they were leery of divulging private thoughts to him, they had exchanged small talk. Perhaps his physical condition was why he seemed more empathetic to the fate of the captives.

When Hetty saw the men lined up for departure, she unhesitatingly approached Hunchy to ask him for a favor. She removed a passport photo from the pocket of her apron and asked him to bring it to Fritz, because she had no other way of saying goodbye. She knew Fritz must be frantic. She had saved that small passport photo of herself for a moment such as this and had kept it securely hidden. Hunchy told Hetty that none of the guards at Vught had been informed as to where the men were going. But he said he would give Fritz the photograph, even though conversation was strictly forbidden.

Later that day, Hunchy told Hetty that he had found Fritz and had given him the photograph. She expressed her gratitude to him for taking such a risk. Hunchy looked surprised to hear that Fritz and she were married. Probably because Hetty looked so young. Or perhaps he had another reason for helping her, because he thought she was single. She thought it was unlikely that Hunchy wanted to risk being reprimanded for breaking a rule. She prayed he had kept his word but assumed the worst primarily because by now she knew that lying was part of Nazi training.

When she returned to her barracks after the two-hour roll call that evening, Hetty could not control her anguish. She could not stop the tsunami of pain, the rivers of grief and torment that were now overwhelming her at the realization that she had lost Fritz. The accumulated pain had gotten the better of her and she began to shake and wail uncontrollably, despite being among a few good friends. Dottie, Martha, Lena, and Lisabelle's friendship meant everything to her.

After her tremors died down, she remembered something that she could do whenever she found herself alone and in pain. When everyone was in their bunks asleep that night, Hetty lay on her side with her enamel cup cradled in her hands, like a makeshift pillow beneath her head. Her breathing had calmed, and she decided she would visit Fritz in The Memory Place for the first time. Hetty and Fritz created it before they parted, as a place of worship where empowerment is the driving force, and manifestation of another world is possible. It was a place where they could go in their mind to find and speak to one another, especially when they were far apart. It was a place to generate hope.

Hetty was now in a dramatic world dominated by fear. But as she enters this sacred place, she has faith and trusts in Fritz's love. She feels it and so she believes it is not an abstract place, but a chamber in the heart where the soul comes to life, where prayers get answered and a Deity can grant any wish. If only she can maintain her beliefs. There, she manages to summon up images of Fritz and those family members and loved ones she misses and so desperately needs.

She recalled how they'd talked of this, and she knew it would help her now. She hashed over and over in her mind whether she could have done something to save Fritz from leaving, but it was useless to do so. All she could do was go to their Memory Place and communicate her love to him there.

After her outburst, a pervasive and almost audible quiet – a blanket of sadness – came across the camp that night. Many women's spouses, brothers, and fathers had been sent away. It took days for the raw pain to subside. Only then could they resume control over their emotions and numb themselves to their anguish. They were stuck in their barracks now with the closure of the sewing shop, and what filled the day was their misery taking up real estate in their minds. Even though they all had acclimated to the new "normal" in the camps, now with the men gone, Hetty thought, they would have to adjust all over again. That is when joining the Philips work group and Hetty's new job gave her the incentive she needed to regain hope.

But now, she and the Philips group were traveling at high speed, headed for someplace far away and foreign. Reliving the last time she had seen Fritz, she decided she was going to stop despairing and pull herself together. She remembered how to rekindle hope in The Memory Place. It was her haven, her divine place. Maybe she would run into him soon after they arrived? She kept telling herself that she would see Fritz again. She was determined.

4

FRITZ, JUNE 1945

SURVIVING

Besides finding Hetty, Fritz decided he would try to get his old job and his beautiful apartment back – all of which had been taken from him. He knew it was wishful thinking to imagine getting any of his stolen property and savings returned. He had high hopes, but low expectations.

Fritz Frankel had been born in Berlin to Dutch Jewish parents. Most of his Jewish family still lived in Germany and had most likely undergone the same persecution he had. It did not interest the Nazis whether or not someone actively observed the Jewish faith. It was immaterial to which of the twelve tribes one belonged or if one was Liberal or Reformed, Orthodox or Hassidic. It did not matter whether someone was raised Jewish or not. All were hunted down. Was it perhaps because of their skills, their wealth, intelligence, or their position in society? Was jealousy the affliction of the Nazis? Or was it a war of hatred, ignorance, and persecution – bullying that had gotten totally out of hand?

The Jews, among others, had been systematically persecuted, rounded up, and eradicated before. Not just in Berlin but everywhere in Germany as well as in other countries the Nazis conquered. Fritz prayed that his family had somehow managed to go safely into hiding. He also hoped that his loved ones in Holland had been able to avoid the concentration camps altogether, because the camps were dark and evil, full of suffering and death.

What he especially wished for was that Hetty had had enough strength and will to survive. He knew that giving up meant certain death. Even though everyone experiences war differently, living in fear takes its toll even when you have faith in mankind. Even when there is faith in God. It is faith in the goodness of man that Hetty had always treasured. That undying faith in goodness was her signature gift to others and in Fritz's mind would ensure great acts of bravery and hope.

Luckily, Fritz believed that goodness prevails even in the worst moments. If it had not been for kindness, luck, and affection among the inmates, and random acts of kindness from an occasional enemy soldier, he probably would not have made it home. There were many moments when luck entered into the equation as a mirror for his steadfast belief in seeing Hetty again. If it had not been for The Memory Place, Fritz might have gone mad. A space allowing intimate and elaborate possibilities, on a spiritual level.

Returning to the Van Dyke's in Amsterdam meant coming home to three unforgettable women – Olivia, Fleur, and Sally Van Dyke. Fritz knew for certain that they would have welcomed Hetty with open arms upon her return. If she were already back in Amsterdam, he knew that the three women would have taken care of her. Knowing that his wife, Hetty Golden-Frankel, was safe would be enough for him. He could almost feel her fingers intertwined with his. He envisioned all of them in the house, waiting for him, together. What joy that image brought him!

Fleur and Sally van Dyke were about Hetty's age. When the war broke out, the two sisters were in their early 20s, having been best friends with Hetty since childhood. Growing up together meant that they were more like family than friends. Their mothers had also been best friends as children. The two families and three generations lived close by one another on the same street, until Hetty's mother, Bertie, had died of cancer six years before the Nazi invasion, in 1934. At that time, Hetty was only 14 years old and her brother, Hans, was one year older. The Van Dyke family had often pitched in to help Hetty's father, Martin Golden, care for her and her brother. Martin had had a tough time mourning the loss of his young wife after her death. It was a great blow to the whole family when Bertie died, yet all were grateful that Bertie had been spared the horrors of the Nazi occupation. Hetty and her brother were close in age and in their relationship, too. This closeness had partly to do with the awareness of seeing Martin at a loss with Bertie gone. Together, they decided to watch over him.

Around the time of Bertie's death, her older sister, Rosalie, and Rosalie's son, Richy, returned from living in America for the purpose of assisting Martin raise his children as a single father. Although there was some talk of an approaching war, they both came back to Amsterdam, and became key figures in Hetty's and Hans's lives. They lived directly upstairs, above the Goldens. Martin had little time due to the demands of his job. He was a concert violinist and pianist who, besides playing in the Concert Hall of Amsterdam's orchestra most evenings, also taught at the conservatory during the day. That is why Aunt Rosalie became the mother in the family, and Cousin Richy like a brother to Hetty. Olivia was like another beloved aunt, and the three families all celebrated festive occasions together as one large family. Martin had gifted Fleur and Sally piano lessons for several years, as well.

Richy and Hetty had worked together at Paramount Pictures in Amsterdam until the war broke out and everything changed.

Fritz joined Hetty's family much later. He had met Martin on the same day he met Hetty, in May 1942, at the family flat in the Jewish

Ghetto. Fritz knew him fairly well, at least until Martin's disappearance. The list of the missing was long. Approximately 40 family members on Fritz's side and about the same number on Hetty's side had disappeared, family by family, sometimes one by one. Fritz did not expect to see many relatives ever again, because they had been taken captive early on, and millions had been known to have perished by now. He hoped to find Hetty's father safe and sound back in Amsterdam. Fritz was always on the lookout for friends, former colleagues, and associates. It was inconceivable to imagine them all gone, and it would take years before he believed all were dead. Brutalized. Murdered, left to perish unattended without graves. He had not met anyone on his way back who had endured more than two years in a camp, and it did not surprise him. How could anyone withstand more?

The Van Dykes had been living at the same address since before the war began. Fritz knew they had all been alive and well at least until June 8, 1943. That day, he and Hetty had been taken captive in the middle of the night, violently abducted from their beds in the dark. He doubted whether the Van Dykes were aware of what had happened to them.

Although the Van Dykes lived nearby, right around the corner, they might not have heard about it. Most night raids began happening systematically in 1942. The Nazis wanted to keep all abductions hidden from witnesses for as long as possible. No one was supposed to see the brutal treatment used when Jews were taken from their homes. The Nazis wanted to avoid confrontations, to fulfill their mission without complications or interruptions.

Trucks carrying armed soldiers patrolled the streets day and night and primarily carried out armed raids of the Jewish neighborhood. Sometimes one family would be taken, sometimes complete streets were barricaded, with hundreds of entire families taken systematically from their homes and bundled into the trucks waiting downstairs. People vanished without warning; there was no opportunity to say goodbye to anyone. Like a well-oiled machine, a sophisticated, planned, sinister eradication of an entire race was taking place. This had continued until the ghetto was empty in November 1943.

Witnesses kept quiet after seeing houses emptied of their residents. Within a week, all belongings, including art, valuables, and furniture had been removed. This was a clear indication to everyone that these people would never be returning. But where had they been taken to? Later the vacant homes would fill up with new residents. For a long time, this strategy of having few or no witnesses worked in the Nazis' favor. It kept their true underlying agenda hidden longer.

For centuries, people who were subject to hostile invaders have experienced violent pogroms – which were savage raids. History books are full of tribal wars going back to the beginning of time. But no one in 1942 was prepared for such a bestial, ethnic cleansing war to take place in modern times, and no one knew how to organize a successful resistance to stop it. A surprise invasion, as air-tight and methodically carried out as this one was, left everyone in Europe unprepared and asking questions. The worst part is that the targeted groups felt no protection from anyone and were constantly anxious, if not terrified. Even the Dutch Jewish Council, created on February 13, 1941, was established to facilitate the Nazis' hidden agenda. The appointed director of the office was to act as a liaison between the Jewish community and the Nazis. Every week, a new restriction was to be implemented, and the Jewish Council was to oversee it.

Not only did Jews go missing in night raids, they were also taken from the streets in broad daylight as early as 1941. Large trucks full of soldiers would round-up anyone at random, it seemed. Several soldiers would stop the truck suddenly in front of a café, enter it, demand to see everyone's papers, and without an explanation, remove certain civilians from the tables where people sat enjoying a drink with friends. This was not only traumatic for those being taken, it was frightening and shocking for the onlookers, too.

On February 25 and 26 of 1941, the general public went on strike to protest the pogrom raids taking place, demonstrating against the persecution of the Jews. However, it ended badly. Although the event was peaceful, the Nazis violently intervened, leaving many dead and many more wounded. As a result, the cities had to pay millions of Dutch guilders to the invading regime, and it was probably the reason that the public stopped organizing rallies. Gathering spots for citizens, like cafés, concert halls, libraries, and work places slowly became dangerous places to be.

Nothing had been the same after that night. The Van Dykes could have thought that Hetty and Fritz might have escaped by train, on foot, or by boat to a neutral country such as Sweden or Switzerland, or that they had gone into hiding somewhere in or outside the city, most likely somewhere in the countryside. Some people bought their way to freedom, and some had help from the Resistance groups who were working hard to undermine the enemy. But there was no way of knowing. It was far safer for the Van Dykes not to know whether Fritz and Hetty had made specific plans – or for them to know theirs. In this way, Fritz believed he could protect everyone best. He had no idea whether Olivia and the girls had fled, been captured, or remained living in Amsterdam on the Amsteldijk.

Hetty (left) and her brother Hans: One of just two photos of them that survived the war. (Private collection)

5

HETTY, JUNE 6, 1944

DAY ONE AT AUSCHWITZ

Daylight was fading when Hetty's train came to a standstill. June rain was pouring down on all sides. The women had arrived somewhere, but the freight car doors remained shut. The women listened, and they heard only muffled voices at first. One woman stood on Hetty's shoulders to see what was going on. There was a train directly across from them filled with people, and a long row of anxious prisoners standing on the platform outside.

One of the Dutch women recognized the language coming from the adjacent train. She happened to understand the Hungarian language and quickly learned the train was full of Hungarians who had been waiting a long time to disembark. They were speaking of their capture and deportation, and they, too, were terrified and starving. However, they seemed hopeful, having no clue as to what was awaiting them. That very day they had been taken from their familiar surroundings and were still dressed in their usual clothing. They still had their personal belongings with them, packed in their suitcases.

These people, primarily Jews, had been traded for money. The Nazis paid the Hungarian government by removing some restrictions and reducing sanctions in exchange for Jewish human freight. The Hungarians had heard through the grapevine on board the train that an Allied invasion had just taken place in Normandy. The Allies had been planning a surprise invasion for some time. This invasion orchestrated in secret between world leaders from several continents was meant to defeat the Nazis and free Europe. That day, June 6, 1944, came to be known as "D-day" – a historical date that will be engraved in the minds of Europeans and history books forever. That is the very day that Hetty's train arrived at Auschwitz.

The battle that started in Normandy, France, would, in reality, last for a few months before the allied forces were actually able to free occupied territory. They arrived by sea and landed on the Western-most beaches of France at Omaha and Juno beach, and they then proceeded East. This was amazing news and confirmed what Hetty had heard on the radio a few days before. A wave of hope floated through the air, lifting everyone's spirits. However, Hetty and her fellow inmates were still in a dire predicament. No one knew how long it would take for the Allied troops to reach them or free Europe, so counting on their help was very uncertain. Hetty felt a surge of hopeful energy as she prayed for a swift rescue. But it was short lived.

Beyond the six consecutive rows of high-voltage barbed wire fencing in the distance, trains approached. Selections of some sort were being made farther down on the platform where Hetty's train had stopped. Her group was forced to wait hours in their parked train.

A Nazi soldier standing with a group of his comrades was commanding the incoming civilians on the platform to go either to the left or to the right. All of these civilians, coming from different places, were, unlike Hetty's group of inmates, coming directly from their hometowns, perhaps having been captured in a night raid. Everyone in Hetty's group had lost their private belongings more than a year ago when they arrived at Camp Vught. She suspected that these new prisoners were about to lose theirs, too.

Just then, a family of six who had traveled together were being separated on the platform. The volume of the voices increased as the family was torn apart, the parents screaming in protest. The Nazis were shouting, beating, and pulling the parents away from their young children, who stood screaming, arms outstretched, their faces transfixed with fear. Then a commanding officer stepped in, and with a calming voice urged the prisoners to follow orders and keep moving. They were told that they would be reunited with their families later after taking showers and being issued sleeping quarters. He spoke almost hypnotically, to prevent this outburst from escalating any further, addressing the mothers and children first and then the men. The women were led to a large building and disappeared from sight. The men went in the opposite direction. The children went somewhere else altogether. Hetty heard the cries become sobs and she started to shake uncontrollably. There were hundreds of people from all walks of life in the line. A line that kept moving and seemed to have no end.

The voices and screams silenced for a moment, the belongings of all of the arrivals remained behind on the platform. They ranged from suitcases with the name and address of the owner neatly written on the side to simple cloth sacks full of possessions, tied with string. Hetty could clearly hear that same commanding voice order a subordinate soldier to gather these belongings and, speaking German, order him to bring all of the luggage to "Kanada."

Although Hetty understood the language, she did not know what Kanada meant. She assumed that the bags would never be reunited with their rightful owners, just as their belongings had never been returned to them in Camp Vught. She saw how unceremoniously the suitcases were handled and placed onto trucks ready to drive away.

The people arriving at Auschwitz who had come straight from their homes were often laden with more than clothing. The Nazis had instructed them to bring a few important possessions, including liquor, cigarettes, money, and valuables – and many thought it was clever to sew precious little things like money and family photos into coat pockets and skirt hems. When these people were, upon arrival, forced out of the trains and brought directly to the gas chambers and killed, their belongings ended up in Kanada, where everything was inspected and sorted. It was calculated robbery. Kanada was the name for the mile-long street of warehouses where the prisoners' stolen property was sent, sorted, and stored for use or profit by the Nazis. It was the German spelling of "Canada," which they saw as the land of plenty.

When the Hungarian train was empty, Hetty saw that her train was next. When the doors opened, they saw countless windowless brick buildings, directly behind which were two tall chimneys reaching high into the skies – sparks and smoke flying out of them in all directions. A chill ran down Hetty's spine as she realized where the stench of searing flesh was coming from. Could this smell be the remains of the first Hungarians they had just seen disembark onto the platform?

All of the women in her wagon were already terrified and stiff from fear, watching the first of their group line up in rows of five and go through the selection process. Impeccably dressed soldiers had assembled at the end of the ramp for the Philips group selection. The first people to manhandle them were male prisoners in striped uniforms. They ordered everyone out of the train, and if they did not get off quickly enough, they yanked the women out by their arms.

"Quick, quick, quick," they ordered, sadistically wielding sticks. These armed men, prisoners themselves, met each train and were given the task of keeping law and order. They had no interest in the plight of the newcomers. They even seemed empowered while beating the women as they came off the train, assigned the task of scaring them into obedience. All the while they shouted obscenities, calling the women whores and scum.

Farther down on the platforms, uniformed Nazi physicians were selecting the human freight. Women between the ages of 16 and 45 were being inspected like cattle. Droopy buttocks, flabby stomachs, and bad skin were signs of malnutrition. The ones with apparent strength were sent over to one side and would most likely become slave laborers and be put to work. Hetty heard one officer instruct the guards to keep twins together for an extra inspection at the clinic. These twins were later used for medical experiments in the Nazi laboratories.

Hetty was appalled to see that exceptionally beautiful women were being sent to a smaller line and given priority. Were those women being selected for working in the brothels? She became transfixed with fear. Why were such small children being pulled out of the line? If a soldier looked at a child in an appraising way, even very young ones, she questioned whether they were being selected for sexual abuse. The children were frantic, screaming and kicking with all their might. Teenagers from around 13 years of age were separated into yet another line. Where would they be put to work? Hetty swallowed, her throat dry.

The women were instructed to undress and stand naked for inspection. She and the 400 women from the Philips group had arrived exhausted, barely able to stumble from the trains, and now as they stood at attention during roll call, they were cold, unprotected, and bewildered. Some were crying because of the physical strain of being without food, water, or medical care for more than 72 hours. For nearly four days they had been inhumanely treated. Their basic needs and cries were being ignored. Even the use of a toilet upon arrival had been refused. Not one ounce of decency was present in the treatment of prisoners at Auschwitz. The result was seeing hundreds and hundreds of prisoners crying and pleading for the normal needs of a human being. This treatment was beyond excessive, it was intentionally sadistic and dehumanizing.

Sharply dressed officers made the rounds and observed them closely. Why were these officers always dressed so well? Their uniforms were starched and well-attended to, the fabric exceptionally sturdy and elegant, and their knee high, black leather boots always buffed to a bright sheen. Their attire was intimidating, especially for the naked women, and Hetty was sure that the soldiers knew this.

At Camp Vught, the women were used to being ogled by the soldiers who passed by at roll call or who walked into the lavatory with them. But this time they were completely naked, and these guards were new to them. Some looked them up and down with a lecherous smirk on their face. Some spit on them. Some cursed. All felt superior to them. They were young, and their immaturity made every degrading word a punch in the stomach. It was a disgusting and harrowing experience.

As these soldiers patrolled the platform, the naked women no longer cared that they were being inspected or stared at. The men paid little attention and did not seem particularly aroused by what they saw. Most of these women were nearly bald, already half-starved, and lacked any kind of sexual appeal.

Later, after the first selection, when they were allowed to don their filthy clothes again, another type of selection took place. They were commanded to answer questions about their background and skills according to the list that accompanied this freight, to determine which women would be put to work. None of these Nazis was ever friendly or kind. They would either shout at or mock the new arrivals. The training must have made them so. "Kill the unworthy and make them suffer up until their death" was the adage that comes to mind. Their voices were always loud, demanding, and hateful. The prisoners were told that they had to do exactly what was asked of them or they would be shot in the head on the spot.

During each inspection, the women held their bowels as best they could, fighting the urge to defecate. It was incredibly difficult standing still for long, with no toilet facilities available to them, and some women just let everything flow. Some stood whimpering. A few women who were menstruating let the blood drip down their legs. What else could they do? They had not been given any sanitary napkins of any kind. They had nothing with them at all. Most women had stopped menstruating due to the stress they were under and had not had a period in months. Hetty still did, but that would soon change. At any rate, at this stage she was already beyond shame. Most of the women had no underwear on and no tissues to absorb the filth nor a place to put one. The stress of camp life and the lack of nourishment caused their bodies to shut down.

They still had not yet been given any food or water. The Philips women stood longing for shelter and some kind of protection, but they received none. The women simply stood still as they were told, silently weeping and accepting whatever fate awaited them. Hetty's mind was consumed with surviving, even though death might come as a relief. Three fleeting thoughts crossed Hetty's mind. One: she was grateful that she did not have children now; two: she was ecstatic to hear that the allies had landed; and three: she prayed that this meant she would soon be rescued. She assumed that the world *did* care about the plight of the innocent victims being slaughtered. Or so she hoped. Another fleeting thought was that it might already be too late for her, but she would keep surviving, her lust for life winning over the inner battle taking place in her thoughts.

6

FRITZ, JUNE 3, 1945

MASS MURDER

Includes Flashback to 1942

As Fritz looked around at the civilians walking along the streets, he thought that many seemed unencumbered by war. He was the opposite, wondering whether they knew the extent to which the Nazis' victims had been tortured. From home, there could be no way of knowing anything for certain. Truth was anomaly. A lie. A frigid story of mass killings and burial pits. Even after many neighborhoods had been replaced with new tenants, and rumors of atrocities and executions were confirmed, no one could begin to imagine the extent of evil that Fritz had himself witnessed and undergone. The brutality that the Nazis and their collaborators had been capable of was completely unprecedented. Later, he would learn that only 5,000 of 102,000 Dutch Jews had survived the war. That is less than 5 percent of the Jewish population of the Netherlands.

The Nazis were waging a war against many races, and one in particular, as well as against other groups – including the disabled. The Nazi ideology included ridding the planet of the "unworthy" through masterminding a process of organized murder that became known as "genocide", a phrase coined for the first time in 1944 by the Polish-Jewish lawyer, Raphael Lemkin. He lobbied to have the word added as a crime in international criminal lawbooks. He had fled Europe in 1941 and a year later heard the British Prime Minister Winston Churchill on the radio tell listeners about the horrors of World War II. Churchill said: "Whole districts are being exterminated. Scores of thousands – literally scores of thousands of Europeans everywhere – are be executed in cold blood and are being perpetrated by the German police troops," and added "We are in the presence of a crime without a name."

Lemkin defines the word he came up with to make these crimes against humanity specific and to the point. His definition is: "the destruction of a nation or of an ethnic group". "Genos" (Greek) means *race, tribe* and "cide" means *killing*. The word has gone through its own evolution. Ethnic cleansing is a practice as old as mankind, yet until now it had been committed, observed, and reported, but not punished. With the addition of the word and its legal implications, massacres in the future could be prevented. The Nazis had singled out Jewish people to blame for society's problems in Europe and had used them as a scapegoat. A clear case of genocide had taken place at an astronomical scale.

For Fritz, the Nazis were people consumed with jealousy and delusions of grandeur. This was the mentality of the German chancellor, Adolf Hitler, who now held the scepter and was commander of the Nazi party since January 30, 1933. Nazi arrogance and superiority seemed a façade for greed, ignorance, and deception. Lying was the modus operandi for the Nazis. Were they not a confederacy of sociopaths? Where was decency? Where was their humanity? Hidden behind the lies they told themselves and broadcast aloud. How does an entire country justify murdering innocent people? Hitler used propaganda to make Germany great again. In the end, he lost the war. Not only had he lost, but he had put Germany to shame and abandoned and impoverished his own people, supporters, and allies. He had caused the people to suffer needlessly and was the reason the economy, culture, and way of life had dissolved.

This war was about killing people and robbing them simultaneously. The Nazi party was amassing a fortune in money, art, jewelry, and all manner of valuables. That the stolen Jewish money paid for the weapons, tanks, ammunition, and in fact the entire war, proved that the entire defiling of Jews was a coverup for an intricately designed heist carried out to make Hitler and his cohorts ever richer.

The Nazis had encouraged the public to watch the many propaganda films they had produced blaming the Jews, Roma, Sinti (a subgroup of the Roma), and others in society considered to be inferior races, for crimes no one had committed. "Roma" is the word that this ethnic group currently uses to describe themselves. Although these people had commonly been called Gypsies during the war years, Gypsy is now considered a derogatory term.

Yet, despite neither the Jews nor any of these other groups having committed crimes, the general public started choosing sides, influenced by Nazi propaganda. Their professionally made films and publications were convincing, full of false claims of wrongdoing on the part of the Jews. In truth, the Nazis were trying to blame these groups for the economic struggles the average German was dealing with. They had been experiencing a decline in living standards due to the stock market crash of 1929. That is when unemployment hit the US, where Germany had their loans based. The decline seemed uncontrolled.

At the same time, Germany was politically unstable, and the people were looking for someone to blame. The country was divided, and Hitler claimed he would singlehandedly unite them. He did this by the use of blame and hatred. The Nazis took power, based on lies. Films were created in such a way as to ostracize innocent people. They became a useful distraction to cover up what was really going on because, in the meantime, the Nazi's themselves were up to treachery, which ultimately included betraying the trust of their allies and robbing their own people of much more than their integrity.

The Nazis needed to convince the public that they, the citizens, would greatly benefit from the Jews' removal so they would be happy to collaborate. By eliminating Jews and stimulating greed, they claimed that all other citizens could get better homes and enjoy increased wealth. Everyone would be getting a piece of the pie, and this would justify the slaughter of millions of healthy, law-abiding citizens.

Armed soldiers patrolling the once peaceful streets of the Netherlands became a terrifying and frequent sight when the war began. Fritz was shocked when his country was invaded. Most Dutch residents kept to themselves and wanted nothing at all to do with the Nazis. They preferred to keep a low profile and so refrained from questioning authority. They conformed to the new rules, somewhat reluctantly, and hoped it would all just go away. The Dutch tried to assume the best: do what they were used to doing in a free country. Much better than assuming the worst. At first, people figured the Nazi occupation was about gaining territory and wealth. A military war. That made sense because Germany had surrendered a lot of land and money after losing World War I, as reparation for the war crimes they had committed; however, by the end of World War II, it was clear that Hitler had had other shocking ideas in mind all along. Hitler, the fascist, delusional leader of the Nazi Party, wanted much more than just land. He wanted wealth, power, and respect. Above all, he wanted to rule the world, annihilate an entire race, and use his victims' money to finance his war. Along with establishing breeding farms, he was well on his way to the creation of a pure, 'Aryan', white privileged race. The rest would have to go.

Hitler was supported by an inner circle of deputies, including Heinrich Himmler (head of the SS), Joseph Goebbels (taken on to head the Propaganda projects), Rudolf Hess (Hitler's personal assistant), Ernst Röhm (appointed head of the S.A. paramilitary unit), Hermann Wilhelm Göring (head of the military), Albert Speer (the Reich's architect), and Martin Bormann (Hitler's second in command).

A few attempts had been made to assassinate those in high command, including Hitler. But because Hitler was paranoid, he had found a way to create competition among his generals. In so doing, he had made it difficult for them to trust one another and plan a coup. None of the many attempts on his life ever succeeded.

Nazi officials were often in the news, and once the killing camps were up and running at full capacity, the diabolic nature of the regime came to light. Yet not everyone realized the scope of the plan – the Nazis aimed to rule Europe and then the Americas and the rest of the world.

Eliminating the Jews would put more money in the hands of a few Nazi-run organizations, like the police, who would have control over everyone. Even German citizens were frightened that this might have unfavorable consequences for them. Hitler's generals may not all have been as fanatical as he was, but they were still fascists, none of whom complained about lining their pockets with the Jewish money that they and the Nazi elite had stolen. They seemingly justified these immoral deeds by spreading and believing the lies they told. Europe had become a narcissistic society run by a narcissist dictator. Jewish gold was also paying the insurance for Vatican protection if need be. An Austrian bishop in the Vatican, Alois Hudal, was a Nazi sympathizer. The Nazis had made a private deal with him, and after the war, he provided the Nazi leaders with needed documents and an escape route out of Germany with escorts to South America.

Meanwhile, some German physicians had been approved by the Nazis to conduct painful and often deadly medical experiments on thousands of prisoners interred in the camps, without their permission. The most notorious of these was Dr. Josef Mengele.

Considering the inhumane conditions, lack of consent, and questionable research standards existing in the camps at the time, modern scientists overwhelmingly reject the use of results from experiments performed there. These experiments centered around three topics: survival of military personnel, testing of drugs and treatments, and the advancement of Nazi racial and ideological goals. After the war, only a few of the biomedical experts who had helped implement and legitimize Nazi racial hygiene policies were ever indicted or disciplined professionally. In fact, many continued their careers in the US, after being brought over by the US government specifically to continue their research. Operation Paperclip was a secret the United States intelligence program kept at the end of World War II, in which more than 1,600 Nazi scientists, engineers, and technicians were paid to work and live freely in the United States.

Germany had become a police state, run by the fascist elite in the 1930s, and Hetty and Fritz and most of the world could do nothing to stop it as they watched fascism unfold. Fascism is a far-right, authoritarian, ultra-nationalistic political ideology and movement characterized by a dictatorial leader. It often appeals to people in tough economic times, because they want a tough leader to protect them from uncertainty. However, fascist protection is an illusion. Fascists want total control of the populace. It has nothing to do with Democracy.

Under the Nazis, Fritz's name had been replaced by a number; he was completely stripped of his identity. Fritz as a person no longer existed, and surviving each dangerous day was not just a challenge but a necessity. Confining Fritz and Hetty and other evicted Jews to ghettos where they were to be permanently removed later on was not only a means to isolate them. It was intended to make them feel trapped like animals. By cutting them off from family members who lived in other towns and prohibiting transportation and imposing restrictions on all of their movements, the Nazis made them feel they were already imprisoned – which they were. This had been the Nazis' objective all along. The daily lives of Jews had become a nightmare, because until the murdering started, cruelty was how the Nazis ruled.

Although the treatment of Jews in the Netherlands was shocking and more than disturbing at the time, Fritz now knew that there was no comparing it to daily "life" in the camps. Breaking the will of the Jews might have been difficult at the beginning of the war, but as time passed, the extreme anger, pain, and sorrow it brought forth would weaken them. The will, heart, and mind of all Jewish communities were under assault. The "Final Solution" to the Jewish Question was the name of the Nazis' plan to eliminate all the Jews in Europe. It had been designed and enforced by the leader of the SS police, Heinrich Himmler. The architect of genocide also had another partner, Joseph Goebbels, the mastermind of the propaganda used to convince the populace that the lies were all true. And he was particularly good at his job. All in all, the ten main generals assisting Hitler were together accountable for the morbid genocide taking place.

7

HETTY, JUNE 1944

DAY TWO AT AUSCHWITZ

Includes Flashback to 1942

The sickening stench of burning flesh once again filled Hetty's lungs, and she vomited. She felt continually nauseated. The Philips women had been standing at attention for 24 hours outside in the pouring rain waiting for roll call, selections, and for the inspections to end. They had not even entered the main camp yet. It had been excruciating. They had not been shown any kindness, brought to sleeping quarters, or gotten sleep of any kind. Everyone arriving at Auschwitz had to endure this kind of sadism. No food had yet been given to them, and although they pleaded for water, their requests were still being refused. They were warned not to touch the faucets anywhere, either, because the water was contaminated. Hetty had obeyed but wondered whether that was just another lie. She was by now used to Nazi cruelty, but she was desperate for water. "They must feed us or at least give us water, mustn't they?" she cried. "How could they be so cruel as to ignore us?" She couldn't swallow anymore; her throat was parched.

Nevertheless, Hetty needed to refrain from giving into the aching need of her body and restrain her companions from trying to get at the faucets. She had learned to act in a certain way at Camp Vught to survive. After all, she was preparing for a career in Hollywood. She had learned to remain silent, whisper, be alert, and keep her eyes roaming for signs of an assault. What was needed was to be good at play-acting, for survival. A more serious part does not exist, she thought. It was a survival mechanism needed to stay alive. She had learned to stay out of trouble, be invisible, and not get unwanted attention from anyone, especially the guards. It was important to always be on good behavior, and never steal food from any of the other inmates (which was a daily practice for many). She would secretly communicate with friends and inconspicuously try to help others when she could. She had gotten good at all of this at Camp Vught; yet she was not so sure whether she could trust anybody or navigate through this hell here at Auschwitz and manage to survive it.

For the first 24 hours, it seemed as though the lives of those arriving hung in the balance. Some of the older women were so weak that they fainted. They would then be dragged away across the muddy square by their feet and arms. Those who collapsed were sometimes shot, and all of them ushered out on their backs. It made Hetty sick to her stomach.

When her sick friend Martha nearly fainted during that first roll call, Hetty had rubbed her back with a fist to keep her from falling down. Hetty and a few of the prisoners who had witnessed the Nazis murdering some new arrivals were commanded to remove the corpses. Although she had not totally recovered from her illness before this horrific transport, she was still strong enough to do what she was told. This was the first time she had encountered death, let alone touched another dead person. It was dreadful. Inside she cringed, but outwardly no trace of her nausea showed. She was a quick learner and used this opportunity to keep a watchful eye on her friends from Camp Vught. Her eyes kept searching everywhere for her brother, her father, her aunts and uncles, her friends, and of course, Fritz. Auschwitz was considerably larger than Camp Vught, and there was no way of knowing where the men were being housed. Hetty felt defeated when she realized this.

After roll call finally occurred, she and the other Philips women had to walk a long way to the area where their assigned sleeping barracks were. As they passed a group of children, a young boy of about 10 years old shoved a sausage into Hetty's hand. Astonished, she looked at it as if it were a foreign object. Despite her raging hunger, she was unable to take a bite, her throat constricting at the thought of swallowing it. Terrified and exhausted, her nausea took over. She was too scared to eat anything. By the time she realized she could not eat it, it was too late. She looked back over her shoulder to thank the boy, but she had lost sight of him.

She quickly passed the sausage on to a stranger in the next row, who stuffed it in her mouth and swallowed it whole. This woman showed Hetty no sign of gratification or gratitude; she was just another walking zombie obsessed with food. Hetty was now witnessing what women look like when they go mad from hunger and thirst.

Chewing or swallowing took more energy than many could spare. At this stage, no one was able to express emotion either, for the same reason. Movement cost a large amount of energy. Talking required more. Although Hetty was fixated on food, at the same time, she could not consider eating; her brain had shut down. She was unable to utter a word or to rationalize why she did not eat the sausage herself. But she, too, was operating on automatic pilot. Her only coherent thoughts had to do with staying alive.

Then, another selection took place. This time they were separating the elderly from the rest before entering the barracks. The selection was led by a very young woman prisoner – a teenager really – assigned the task of managing the women's barracks and controlling them. Her role was called a Kapo. The pattern of humiliating prisoners was evident on her face. She seemed to live in a disassociated space. At every opportunity, she said something sadistic to the prisoners. This young girl had been horribly abused by the Nazis and, after being incarcerated for a long time, was as inhospitable and cruel to the Philips women as the Nazis had been to her. She behaved as a commander, shouting orders and whipping the women with her stick. She appeared to be taking out all her pent-up anger toward her own captors on the new captives. She was angry because the Philips group was not required to go inside the camp, and this meant that for some reason they were privileged. It also meant she had more people to watch and manage.

When one person timidly asked her why they had no food or water, she shouted at the women, accusing them of being special cargo, while hitting them to make them move faster. She said that most trains into the camp sent prisoners directly to the gas chambers. Most were killed upon arrival and never even spent a single night there. Those who survived were to be put to work. "Why bother giving you food or water when you will be dead soon enough?" she said. "What would be the point?" This guard said that there were thousands of deaths every day. After scolding the women and luring them to drink the contaminated water, she administered a horrible blow that crushed the women's hope altogether. She told them that *any relatives who had preceded them to Auschwitz were already dead. There was no hope of ever seeing them again!*

The Philips women broke down and cried again, but in a new way, this time. They were sobbing inconsolably, having heard this heartbreaking news of their loved ones. The guard stared back at them coldly, entirely unconcerned. The women's misery took flight. Wailing soared, and other guards had to join the teenager to help quell the uproar. They hit the women hard and then whipped them even harder, ordering the sobbing to stop.

At Auschwitz, the only thing the prisoners still owned was their bodies. The only thing the Nazis valued was whether somebody was fit enough to use it. The enslaved captives were to be put to work for up to 12-hour shifts. Prisoners were a product, judged only by the skills and stamina they presented.

After the sobbing had died down, the young Kapo told them that whatever misery they were experiencing had no comparison with hers. She was from the Balkans and had already been in Auschwitz for two full years. Here, she had personally witnessed the deaths of her parents and the rest of her family. Immediately afterward, she had been selected to be a sexual plaything for a Nazi soldier. He had taken her virginity at 12 years old, kept her locked up, and had then passed her on to lesser officers once he had tired of her. Then she had been assigned to women's barracks.

Her only surviving brother, Moni, had also been sexually abused; gay pedophile Nazis had used him as a toy at the age of eight. They had turned him into a child prostitute who, after being passed from man to man, had ultimately been murdered when he ceased to amuse the Nazi soldiers. Most of the children and young adults used in this way never survived. Moni had been used up, neglected, starved, had contracted a disease, sent to the gas chambers, and was now dead.

This broken teenage guard stood with her stick in hand and looked utterly devastated. She had just recently heard of her baby brother's death, the last words of her story coming out in a sob. Then she slowly took hold of herself, straightened, and within a few short moments the women saw her transform back into the raging maniac again.

Hetty was so frightened. How could human beings do these things to other human beings? She never could have imagined that these stories were true; however, since setting foot in Auschwitz, she definitely could. There was evil in every inch of this place, and she started shivering again. Auschwitz was a bottomless pit of Hell on Earth.

She herself had also been lied to, misled, robbed, beaten, starved, isolated, and punished. Even when she had worked for the Escotex corporation sewing as a slave laborer in Camp Vught, she had lived with daily fear of punishment. But here, anything was possible, and it seemed that life could not get much worse. She remembered how she had hated Camp Vught when they were interned there, but now she could only long for the days when she could count on seeing Fritz daily and feeling his love.

8

FRITZ, JULY 1945

BREEDING THE PERFECT RACE

The long hours spent sitting on the truck had given Fritz time to try to understand how the Nazi ideology had taken hold to such an extent that it had allowed normal people to go along with the genocide that the Nazis were committing.

Nazi ideology emphasized the superiority of a so-called "Aryan" race. This alleged superior race was also found in Germany and the Netherlands, but it was possible to breed future generations of Aryans everywhere. Breeding farms were part of the entire system of "racial improvement," termed "eugenics." Eugenics is an ideology that has reared its ugly head throughout history. Ethnic cleansing by means of genocide is the desired way to achieve a perfect society. Eugenics played a significant role in how World War II was conducted, first in Germany and later elsewhere. It was initially a well-kept secret known to only a select few.

The adage, "Remove the unwanted and cultivate the wanted," applied to the process. Some of Hitler's generals were even more fanatical than he was. Hitler himself did not have the physical features that an Aryan society required. Yet, this society would be run by Hitler himself, although not all of Hitler's supporters were supportive of the ideology nor the manner in which Hitler's plan was to play out. Early on there were suspicions that his ideology was born from repressed homosexual desires. Display of homosexuality and transsexual behavior was unacceptable at the time. Perhaps Hitler's inner wish to be gay fueled an outward display of denial, which is not an uncommon reaction to emerging desires unacceptable to society.

In the early 1930s, German scientists had been sent to America to study eugenics for the purpose of forced sterilization. It is there that German scientists observed how best to forcibly control population growth. In 1933, sterilizations began in Germany. Doctors in the German countryside were asked to report the backgrounds of their patients and monitor the children resulting from mixed marriages. They were told to select children of about the age of 13 whose dark features and tinted skin were not in accordance with the desired Aryan features. A few thousand German youngsters underwent required sterilization before they became sexually active.

There were Aryan breeding farms in Germany, where "racially pure" German women were recruited to become breeding partners for German SS (Schutzstaffel) blond officers, the elite paramilitary guard of the Nazi regime, who had grown from being Hitler's bodyguards to a well-trained and aggressive police force that ran most camps. This Lebensborn program, established in 1935, had been the brainchild of Heinrich Himmler, one of Hitler's deputies. He wanted to combat the falling German birthrate while at the same time increasing the number of "racially pure" individuals in the population. The women were sometimes forced to be used as baby-making machines, and the children were taken from them at birth to be raised elsewhere in a controlled environment. Meanwhile, undesirable races needed to be eliminated. Himmler referred to Jews and other non-Aryan people as "subhuman."

Tens of thousands of disabled and mentally challenged people in institutions also underwent forced sterilization. Or death. Many infants and children were murdered. Doctors were complicit. Most institutions were emptied, and the residents deported. In fact, the first people to be slaughtered at Auschwitz were not Jews. That concentration camp was initially established to kill disabled and mentally challenged children. Healthy young people were sometimes sterilized because their appearance was not Aryan enough.

Doctors would give flimsy excuses to parents of children with learning difficulties or disabilities, saying they needed to be sent to sanatoriums to "get well." Yet, many children were intentionally killed there, the doctors telling the parents that their child had died due to natural causes. The patients were systematically given lethal injections with the consent of psychiatrists and doctors who thought that ridding the world of these lesser individuals was the right thing to do. The Nazi ideology convinced many citizens to not only agree, but to participate in mass murder. A conspiracy theory gone sour.

The Nazis also created a summer sport camp for young boys. There, they were groomed, trained, and force-fed lies to emphasize loyalty to a perverse ideology. These boys would become the next generation of Aryan military, willing to fight to the death. They were brainwashed to believe a number of antisocial myths and to hate the Jews. These young boys of approximately 13 years of age were often tall, with light blond hair, blue eyes, high cheekbones, and an athletic stature, all of whom were White, of course. Loyalty to the regime was the goal. Only this combination of features was desirable, and these children were together called the *Hitler Jugend* (the Hitler Youth). The young girls' organization was called the *Bund Deutscher Mädel,* the Association of German girls, founded in June 1930.

Swaying the populace to accept this hatred of Jews and the building of an Aryan race was achieved in the 1930s partly by using the propaganda film, *The Eternal Jew*, which became required viewing in the theaters in the Netherlands and abroad (similar to how social networking works on TikTok, X, Instagram, or any other social media channel, the spreading of a conspiracy works best when information goes viral.) Of course, this ruling came after the Jews were no longer permitted to enter theaters or public buildings. There were also documentaries made in which false claims were used to blame the Jews for Germany's defeat in World War I.

Hitler had fought in World War I. After Germany lost, but before he became the newly elected party leader, he was thoroughly enraged when he saw parts of Germany being sold off as part of the reparations for Germany's war crimes during World War I. He used his position to ignite nationalism once again, proclaiming he wanted to "make Germany great again" after its humiliation at the end of the last war.

By the end of 1938, propaganda had made headway in heightening the fascist ideology among the German people. Fritz had witnessed the rise of Hitler as he was broadcast on the radio, but somehow Dutch citizens felt protected by the fact that they were a small, unassuming country that had managed to remain neutral during World War I. They assumed that this neutrality was still in effect, as it had been for many years. The Dutch had not expected to be anything but neutral, nor expected to choose sides in the case of an impending war. That naiveté would cost the country their freedom and most of the Jewish population their lives. The Dutch were not prepared to be invaded and subject to a dictator. Although Hitler was elected, he ran the country from a totalitarian world view. No one was prepared for the onslaught that followed.

Hitler's first political party, the German Workers' Party, was formed in 1919, right after the flu pandemic of 1918 had killed millions and World War I just ended. This pandemic had left a terrible scar on the people of Europe as well as a psychological trauma on those who survived. The party grew into the National Socialist German worker's Party, or Nazi Party, by 1920. Some Dutch countrymen would join a similar party in the Netherlands. Hitler, under the influence of a group of occultists in Vienna during his college years, was convinced of his own ideology and was an advocate of using force to get whatever he wanted. He had been convicted of treason in 1924 for trying to overthrow the Weimar government in what became known as the Beer Hall Putsch, though he was imprisoned at Landsberg for only eight-and-a-half months of his five-year sentence.

While imprisoned, he wrote a manifesto, *Mein Kampf*. In this lengthy document he blames the Jews for all the problems of the world, in general, and for Germany's problems in particular. He climbed the ladder of success from being a popular speaker to becoming the head of the Nazi party and Chancellor of Germany. His charisma and oratorial skills accounted for his ability to mobilize the masses. He became interested in propaganda, too. This is the tool that best spreads any desired conspiracy theory.

Hitler became very popular because of the grand promises he made to the German people. Many citizens were disillusioned by the Weimar government's inability to improve the economy, although conditions were similar worldwide. Later, Hitler would become their worst nightmare. He was not only responsible for the madness that murdered millions of his own citizens, but he also singlehandedly allowed the bombing of Berlin and would not surrender to the Allies, even though the deal would have benefited German citizens. He and his destructive personality caused havoc in Germany when he abandoned all of his countrymen and killed himself instead of facing his defeat.

Hitler resented Jews in high places, especially those in positions of power. He had grown up in a remote Austrian town where he had never even heard of the Jewish religion. According to his writings in *Mein Kampf*, he predicted how he would win votes by promising better living conditions and higher salaries, none of which he accomplished when in office. When he lived in Vienna, he lived in the Jewish Quarter, which is where he claimed he had acquired a distaste for everything Jewish. He especially resented the power acquired by Jews owning the main newspaper in Vienna. That is when his ambitions grew; he wanted that power for himself. Hitler had been devastated about not being accepted to the art school he was passionate about attending. He did not handle rejection well, even back then. Nonetheless, he was later able to sell some of his architectural drawings.

His art dealer was Jewish, as was the physician who tended to his mother who was dying of cancer, to whom he supposedly had given heartfelt thanks. But after his time as a soldier in World War I, Hitler became envious of the Jews' close-knit community, intellect, and wealth, and he tried to convince everyone else to resent them as well. Jealousy of the Jews has been the most often recorded reason for Jewish persecution throughout history, because many Jews had achieved prominence, influence, and financial success. Seen historically, the Jews were often expelled from places where they had settled, thereby being forced to live as nomads. It seems to be in their DNA to desire a homeland where they can live in community with God and in peace with their neighbors.

After writing *Mein Kampf*, Hitler's ambitions grew even more. His desire for power became an obsession. He began a campaign to discredit Jews by spreading lies, to make them a scapegoat for the covert operations that he was designing. Although he would encounter opposition and resistance over the years, Hitler would ultimately get his way. In speeches broadcast abroad, Hitler openly blamed the Jews for manipulating the masses. He even blamed Jews for Communism, which was unbelievable to many and would make his absurd case even stronger. He gave the German soldiers and the general populace permission to rebel against Jews and promoted the use of violence, such as what happened in Germany during *Kristallnacht* (the night of broken glass) in November 1938, before the war broke out, which involved the violent destruction of more than 1,000 Jewish stores and businesses while ransacking and looting Jewish property.

Although Hitler considered the leaders of Bolshevism to be his greatest rivals, he believed that if he could convince the Soviet Union to also blame the Jewish people for their own problems, he would gain the leverage he needed to enact a secret plan. His scheme included betraying the Soviets who were under the leadership of Joseph Stalin. Germany had already annexed Austria and Poland and had partnered with other fascist countries, like Italy and Hungary. Hitler's lust for power knew no limits. Although he had gathered together a strong group of powerful allies, called the Axis powers, he eventually broke his promises to some of them and invaded their countries as well.

The Nazis had begun building concentration camps by the late 1930s, before the war, and sent prisoners to be detained there. By 1939, many German Jews were being expelled from Germany and sent away to live in work camps. There were three such Dutch camps in the towns of Vught, Amersfoort, and Westerbork. These were work and transit camps, which meant that all prisoners were destined to be moved to a concentration camp later on. Some Jewish men were allowed to live if they were married to non-Jewish (gentile) women and agreed to undergo a vasectomy to prevent them from reproducing. They were treated terribly and would be cut off from family and friends.

Although Jews were arriving regularly in the camps, the camps were not ready for them. The housing was incomplete, often with floors and windows missing. The Jewish forced laborers had to live in abominable conditions while being made to build the extermination camps and gas chambers themselves. What was worse is that they were also forced to lead many of the new arrivals into the gas chambers and assist in the removal of dead bodies afterward.

As time went on, the Dutch people became more polarized – and Hitler worked to polarize them even further. And that is when everything began to fall apart in Fritz's world. Although only about ten percent of the Dutch population chose to support the NSB, the Dutch faction of the German Nazi party, the rest of the population managed to turn their heads the other way. One hateful plan the

Nazis implemented was hiring bounty hunters to find people in hiding. These were regular Dutch citizens, paid to turn in Jews for the equivalent of 15 guilders a week, with 7.50 guilders for each Jew captured. Some 9,000 Jewish men, women, and children were betrayed. In one instance, a couple of bounty hunters traveled for days to capture little three-year-old Floortje Citroen, a girl who had been sent by her parents to live in a safe house. She was gassed soon after at the Sobibor death camp.

On July 15, 1942, Jewish transports began, mainly of children. The next phase of war was now underway, and from then on, deportations occurred weekly. Because Jews were no longer permitted to be outside their homes after 8 p.m., and they were prohibited from buying food from non-Jewish vendors, they were being slowly but systematically starved and removed.

Even non-Jews – primarily well-educated young adults – were considered a threat to the Nazi regime because they were more likely to challenge the new government. They had been removed from society earlier, mostly by being plucked from the streets during raids, never to surface again. Fritz had learned that the removal of personal freedoms and rights is essential for a hostile takeover. Other important steps included infiltration, segregation, isolation, violence, starvation, abduction, incarceration, and elimination.

Luckily for Fritz, he knew heroes who had helped house and hide Jews. Hundreds of cells working together in the Resistance were able to undermine, spy on, and inhibit many of the Nazis' plans. Hundreds of citizens offered to help and did. But the climate of tolerance that had existed for decades in the Netherlands was over. Anyone could be a traitor, and no one was to be trusted.

9

HETTY, JUNE 1944

DAY THREE AT AUSCHWITZ

As the Philips women listened to the teenage guard tell her story, they could not comprehend what was being said. Could it be true? Were their families really already dead? This was unfathomable. They were in shock and overwhelmed. No wonder that their sobbing and worry increased, tormented by the reality of their predicament. From the time that Hetty had first been incarcerated, she had never experienced cruelty to this extent. Everything had been taken from them. Even their families. Incomprehensible savages, she thought. Would anyone ever be held accountable for the horrific atrocities taking place?

Hetty was instantly catapulted to a new level. She was determined to go on living so that she could tell the world the true story of what happened in the savage massacre of millions of innocent citizens. Only an eyewitness who had undergone and survived such savagery could give a first-hand perspective and testify in the courts. She now knew that she must warn others of what had taken place here, and say, "never forget it, because it could happen again, and it could happen to you."

Hetty had at least found a few of her Philips Group girlfriends again. They had been standing in other lines at roll call. Lena, and her daughter, Lisabelle, 14 years old, had also survived the nightmare of the transport, though Lisabelle had looked very weak, despondent, and pale. Lena had appeared distraught, particularly when she and Lisabelle had been assigned to separate barracks, but she brightened when she spotted Hetty. Although Hetty couldn't do much, she had smiled back when she saw them. In that smile was relief that they had made it this far.

Most of the women were beyond hunger now, exhausted, cold, miserable and close to giving up. One woman decided to run for it and ran straight into the electrified barbed wire fence, its high voltage coursing through her body, causing it to spasm and fry. It took only an instant before she fell to the ground, dead. Hetty was appalled, and her hands spontaneously flew upwards covering her lips. For a moment she understood death. It is a fleeting moment in life; it takes but an instant to end all days. When the guards saw more potential runners opting for suicide, shots were fired to stun the onlookers. They knew they, too, would be shot down along with anyone standing still near them. Hetty understood why someone might take their own life, but suicide was not in her nature. Her lust for life wouldn't allow it. At this moment it became evident that the enemy wanted to be the one deciding who would die, how, and when. So brutal and defining, she thought. She had so much life ahead of her to live for. For the last few days all she had seen was death and abuse – needless, unfair, criminal killing – and she too had had a moment when she hoped to expire along with them.

Once inside the barracks, Hetty and her companions were surprised to see the barren, wooden bed-stays waiting for them. The barracks was a huge warehouse designed to house about 200 prisoners each, but in reality, they sometimes held over 700 people, making it vastly overcrowded inside. Most of the bed-stays were occupied by women from Eastern European countries, primarily Hungary, which accounted for their different way of dressing and speaking. They wore headscarves and were used to working the land. It soon became obvious to Hetty that the majority of these women had no education. Many of the guards, too, both men and women, looked like they were still children. They also seemed uneducated and incapable of expressing themselves, let alone handling the power given them. Here, Hetty was confronted with her first experience of class differences, and restoring harmony in this conflict-ridden place was going to require more wisdom than she possessed at the moment.

Between the rows of bunk beds were benches on which women who had already been interned but had no work had sat for weeks. For some reason, they had not been put to work or slain, but only sat handing out instructions and telling newcomers gruesome stories of what to expect at Auschwitz. Hetty could not believe what they were saying about the number of murdered souls.

She decided that trying to learn some practical tips from these women might increase her chances of surviving here. She listened carefully to conversations in Dutch, German, French, and English. These were mostly women whom Hetty would not normally have conversed with or befriended, and there was no comparing these conversations with those she would have had with her Dutch comrades. But they were all experiencing the same brutality from the Nazis, and these women had already been hardened by the life here. Hetty ultimately found their tips useful.

The rows of three-tiered, seemingly endless, wooden bunk-bed shelving were just deep enough for a person to lie in, their head hanging over the wooden plank and into the aisle. Six women were expected to fit into one hard, wooden compartment each. There were no mattresses at this point, not even straw; only hard bunks built from bare wood. Some of the women had to figure out how to climb up into the top level, the only ladders being at each end of the row of bunks.

The putrid odor in the barracks was similar to the cattle car they had arrived in. The whole place stank of human debris. The women had not yet been brought to a lavatory or given any chance to relieve themselves. It was obvious that nearly everyone had let the urine flow because they could not hold it in any longer. There were only a few pails in the barracks for the purpose, placed in the aisles between bunks, which were already overflowing. A few women were ordered to empty them of the blood, urine, and feces they contained, and clean up what had spilled over. People were nauseous from it. There was no saying "no" to a clean-up command, even if it came from a young guard still in her puberty. It was a scene from hell. The many Kapo guards watched the prisoners suspiciously. Hetty wanted to just lay down, curl up, and sleep. If she died in her sleep, it would probably be better than living one more day in this nightmare. She had come to expect she would die here and wondered whether that would be a relief compared to the continual struggle taking place all around her, as well as in her mind.

Then, some guards approached with scissors. Most of the women arriving at Auschwitz had had their heads shaved, their hair thrown on a large pile; however, because Hetty's group was "the Philips women," their hair was not shaved, only cut very short. Most prisoners at Auschwitz, as in other German camps, had all the hair on their bodies cut off or shaved during induction. This procedure was for "reasons of hygiene" and for escape prevention. The guards had been directed to collect the prisoners' hair so they could sell it for industrial use. Even the hair of women killed in the gas chambers was recycled. At the Belzec, Sobibor, and Treblinka extermination centers they had their hair cut off before they entered the gas chambers, but at Auschwitz the hair was sheared from corpses. The hair obtained in this manner was then disinfected, dried, packed in sacks, and sold to German companies as raw material for haircloth and felt.

Lena was beside herself with worry when she saw how upset Lisabelle was about having her hair cut off. It was devastating for a teenager to have her beautiful long hair stolen like that. Hetty whispered to Lena, "How could these bastards do that to these youngsters, too?" Hetty tried to console Lena, but it was impossible.

Anyone who still owned shoes was required to turn them in. Then the Kapo guards led them to the showers. Hetty's feet seemed barely able to drag her along as she wondered whether these were going to be real showers with water coming out of the faucets. Or would they turn on the deadly Zyklon B gas instead? Were these the gas chambers Hetty had heard about? Or just regular showers? But she desperately needed a shower after that disgusting transport.

When they turned on and she found real water coming out of the faucets, she nearly collapsed in relief. The water was icy cold and there was no soap, but everyone was grateful for the chance to rinse off some of the filth that had been stuck to their skin for days. There were no towels either; they had to drip dry in front of broken windows with gusty winds and torrential rains outside. Each woman was then handed a uniform of dull gray, flimsy, full-length pants, a blouse, and clogs. And nothing fit.

Finally, after going through the 24-hour roll call and inspections and having their hair cut off, they were brought to a large hall where they were issued one bowl of so-called soup, composed of potato peels floating in saltwater. One bowl and one spoon were allotted for six people. Some never got a single spoonful, and the competition for food was a grueling reality. Naturally, with all the fighting over food, some soup spilled onto the floor. Some bowls were quickly slurped up by a single person, and battles began over it, people shouting angrily. Six women with no eating utensils had to find a way to evenly divide one hunk of bread into six portions, otherwise hell would break loose.

Although there were large clear barrels holding water just across from the barracks, its access was refused to them.

Escape was impossible. There were armed guards and watchtowers everywhere. Then there was the omnipresent smell. Tall smokestacks reaching high into the sky emitted the stench of burning hair and flesh 24 hours a day. This is what triggered Hetty's adrenaline rush of angst the most. Even within the first few hours at Auschwitz, it was clear to Hetty that this camp had been built for the purpose of extinguishing human life, reducing humans to vile vermin, untamed and hysterical, until their death by force in gas chambers. They were treated as rodents who had no feelings, no culture, no dignity, as if they already did not exist. This camp was an otherworldly killing machine, and when Hetty was finally assigned a cubicle for resting, she could not escape her own thoughts long enough to get some sleep.

These hard wooden bed-stays were barely large enough for three women, let alone six women who were forced to lay together. How could anyone get sleep lying like that? If one person needed to climb out or change position, the entire group was forced to adjust. Rats scurried around feeding off the human filth, and there was loud chatter at all hours in a wide variety of languages. Certainly no one could live long in this vile place.

While lying on her uncomfortable bunk, she could only escape to her Memory Place for a few moments at a time, wracked by regrets about what she felt she should have done when the war began. She was mortified that she had once been convinced to obey the Nazis' command to appear at their headquarters in Amsterdam when she was summoned in July 1942. But something amazing had happened the day before, call it a 'divine intervention,' something that would change the course of her life and save her.

10

FRITZ, JUNE 1945

SALLY'S SECRET

Includes Flashback to 1941

Fritz was almost back home, driving along the Amstel, sitting exposed on the flatbed truck, wishing and praying that Sally had succeeded in protecting her family throughout the war. Sally Van Dyke had done something unthinkable to defy the Nazis in January 1941. Fritz did not know whether Sally's secret had come to light or if someone may have found out and betrayed her.

About two months after the invasion, on July 1, 1940, restrictions began to be put on certain people. At first, no one knew why, but these restrictions had primarily targeted people of the Jewish faith. Sally was half Jewish, so this alarmed her and made her watchful. At first, the Jews began to be segregated from the rest. Then they were not allowed to mix or mingle with non-Jews anywhere. Jews could no longer work for gentiles or have gentiles in their employ. Signs were hung throughout the city stigmatizing them, with the words "Jews prohibited" or "Jews unwanted". Plenty of people protested but their dissent was met with an iron fist. Therefore, the Jews became increasingly isolated.

Then, months later, and after many new restrictions had been already imposed, a new law was introduced in January 1941 requiring every Jew to register. Sally looked into what this meant for her and her sister, Fleur. She had always believed she was half Jewish because her father wasn't Jewish. But the Nazis created new criteria for determining who would be considered full-blood and who wouldn't.

The Nazi counsel had decided that even if someone was born of a mixed marriage, he or she was required by law to answer questions regarding lineage. This was done by declaring the faith of previous generations. The past three generations counted on the female side because, in accordance with Jewish tradition, if the mother is Jewish, all of her children automatically are Jewish, too. This is based on the fact that one's mother is certain, but one's father is not. The Nazis needed to establish a new rule to clear up any doubt. In the case of a half-blood child, when there were two Jewish maternal grandmothers, the child (i.e., Sally and Fleur) would then be considered full-blood Jewish and ultimately treated as such. It was now clear that there was good reason to be afraid.

Sally had only discussed this with her own family and with her closest friends, Hetty, Hans, and Martin Golden. When German colleagues had joined her department in the archives at the City Hall, no one was alarmed or suspected infiltration. After the invasion, the Nazis had kept a low profile for a short while, appearing to be agreeable to both governmental and civilian demands. They had infiltrated city hall intentionally. They studied the constitution and the Dutch law books and discovered a way to change the laws to their advantage. By nullifying all papers and agreements, Jews would not be protected under Dutch law any longer. This trick was applied to all European countries conquered by the Nazis. Infiltrate, then change the laws by executive order and make deportation legal.

During the phase of infiltration and before the invasion, the Nazis were able to determine who would be rewarded for collaborating and who would need to be eliminated when the time came. Sally overheard disturbing rumors. Some of her own Dutch colleagues were openly collaborating, which meant they would assist in the witch hunt against Jews.

That is when she realized that the real Nazi objective had to be ethnic cleansing. What was taught in history lessons about eugenics in the past was foreign to Dutch citizens who had never experienced this before. Most had probably never lived in an occupied war zone either, nor learned what it was like to be watched by the invasive eye of an enemy invader. Jews and non-Jews alike were in a constant state of worry and fear. Most people thought only about saving themselves and their families. "There is no blame in that, is there?" Sally wondered.

She would later change her mind about that, believing that people should stand up for the innocent ones who are being wrongly persecuted. She was convinced that, if everyone believed this, many more heroes would stand up and offer a helping hand to save somebody from the Nazis. In return, they would also be saved or benefit in some clear and deserving way. She also thought about all the various religions that proclaim, "love thy neighbor," and how abandoning one's principles works both ways: "if you turn your back on your fellow person in need, the tables will turn on you. The adage, "treat others as you yourself wish to be treated," is a holy truth.

Because Sally had access to City Hall archives in the registration department, she made up her mind to change her family's records. Doing this might be a fatal risk. But it would be worth it if she did not get caught and could save her mother and sister. She waited until late one night when everyone was gone. Entering the archives with her badge, she destroyed all evidence that her mother and grandmothers belonged to the Jewish faith. When the time came to submit her registration form, Sally denied having ever congregated with Jews.

Olivia Van Dyke had, from the beginning of the war, acted like she wasn't Jewish. After Sally altered the records, there was no more connection to her Jewish heritage. Sally remained alert, though. If the enemy ever examined her records closely, she knew what would happen.

Fritz remembered this as he envisioned Hetty at home with the Van Dykes now. Amsterdam is where their love had started. Dead or alive, she still had a strong presence in his mind. Every day, all day, Hetty was around him, always giving him the courage and purpose he needed to go on. He had often needed her during his captivity, and, late at night when he lay in his bunk, he would find her safe and sound in The Memory Place. That place was sacred. It resided in both mind and heart. It is where Hetty had eternal life.

In the Nazi universe, human life itself had no value. The Nazis showed little regard for any humans. This is evident because the desire to create a perfect Aryan race can only be born of dissatisfaction with the human race as it is. Thus, it follows that all others must be considered inferior. Any groups of people that deviate from Aryan perfection is in accordance with the misanthropic dislike of mankind. Whether this came from primitive thinking alone, or insecurity, or fear, or all of the above became evident at the end of the war. Because the arrogant, destructive treatment of humankind can turn around and destroy the predators themselves. Those German people who agreed with the hostile takeover of the world had seemingly lost sight of reason and decency, slowly getting trained to be more and more aggressive, closed-minded, and conservative, and they would eventually find out that the human universe will not allow it. Fritz was always aware that if the ideology goes against the existence of humankind, the aggressor will lose in the end. There is no morality in that.

Anyone who posed a threat to the Nazi regime, including doctors, politicians, lawyers, journalists, students, radicals, and intellectuals had also disappeared. Many went into hiding or joined the

Resistance to help mastermind a way to overthrow the invading enemy. If the identity of a protestor or Resistance member had been compromised this person would need to go into hiding, just like all of the persecuted. If the Nazis came looking for a blacklisted person who had vanished, close family members were at risk. There were acts of terror and formal executions taking place on the streets for all citizens to see. The invaders constantly reminded their captives who it was that had authority and who would pay for rule breaking. Life and death were at the discretion of the Nazis.

The new regulation requiring Jews to register, implemented eight months after the takeover, had not been the first restriction imposed upon the Jewish community. The new rules started off as simply intrusive, but they worsened over time. Two months after the invasion, in July 1940, the first of many restrictions was introduced: the expulsion of Jews from the Dutch Air Force. Then, October 5, 1940, the Germans required all government employees to sign the Aryan Declaration, which stated that they, their parents, and their grandparents had never been part of a Jewish community. The High Court knew that this conflicted with the Dutch Constitution, yet it was permitted, and the Jewish C.E.O. of that institution was expelled. More restrictions followed:

- On October 22, 1940, all Jewish businesses were required to register.
- On November 21, 1940, all Jews employed by the Dutch Government were fired.
- On January 8, 1941, Jews were no longer allowed entrance to movie theaters.
- On January 10, 1941, all Jewish citizens were required to register, even if only one of their grandparents was Jewish. *This is the law that Sally had feared most.*
- On February 5, 1941, all Jewish doctors and lawyers were ordered to register and no longer could have business dealings with people other than those of the Jewish faith.

- On February 11, 1941, restrictions were imposed on Jewish college students.
- On February 13, 1941, The Jewish Council was founded by the Nazis in many occupied countries to provide information on Jews and help impose restrictions accordingly. The Council encouraged the Jewish populace to comply with Nazi demands, warning that if they did not, they might be subject to harsher measures. *This had been a fatal mistake.*
- On February 27, 1941, Jewish people were no longer allowed to donate blood.
- On April 2, 1941, Jewish people were no longer allowed to stay in hotels or guest houses, or even change addresses without permission.
- After April 15, 1941, Jews had to forfeit their radios to the Nazis.
- On April 23, 1941, signs appeared all over The Hague and Amsterdam at random, stating "Jews not wanted."
- On May 15, 1941, no Jews were allowed to play in an orchestra. *That meant that Martin Golden lost his income.*
- After May 31, 1941, no Jews were allowed in parks or swimming pools.

The Jewish people had been taken hostage in their own city.

Between August 8 and 11, 1941, Jews were required to register and relinquish all their valuables (including art collections), property, and bank accounts to Bank Lippmann, Rosenthal & Co, which was founded by the Nazis in the Netherlands in the guise of an existing Jewish bank. The existing bank had been taken over and the management fired. That meant that when the Jews deposited their money and valuables in this bank, it was easily looted by the Nazis.

- On August 8, 1941, segregation of Jewish and non-Jewish children began at school.

- On September 1, 1941, only three weeks later, the Jewish children were no longer permitted to attend school at all.
- On November 28, 1941, Jews were required to pay rent even when they owned their own houses and property.
- On May 3, 1942, the newly installed government forced Jews to purchase and wear a yellow Jewish Star of David on all their garments, underwear, and coats. Thereafter, they would easily be identified, bullied, and ostracized.

Olivia, then in her sixties, was too stubborn for her own good. She refused to wear the Star of David. She was not willing to sign any forms that would incriminate her. She would lie, if need be. And she would fight, even if it sounded foolish for a woman in her sixties, because she was a force to be reckoned with.

Anyone forced to sign a "willingness to emigrate" declaration unknowingly signed away their right to protest later and they were not allowed to change their mind once they had signed it. By "willingly" boarding trains during the deportation, they had legalized their own expulsion and given away all of their rights. Fritz realized that this was the way in which murder was made "legal" by the Nazis. Eventually, Jews were denied participation of any kind in society. Fritz recalled that Olivia wouldn't comply with any part of it. He had often wished that both he and Hetty had not complied, either. They could have had papers forged.

In hindsight, Fritz understood why the restrictions were presented in the manner they were. The frequency and the severity of regulations increased gradually, so as not to reveal the intention, the strategy, and the timeline that Nazi leaders had in mind. In 1942 alone, there were a total of 38 restrictions, including some that forced Jews to hand over their telephones. From a certain date, all forms of transportation, including cars, were no longer permitted for Jews. Although all citizens were living in a state of fearful apprehension, the restrictions for Jews were severe and hinted of worse things to come. Jews could no longer obtain travel permits and were evicted from their homes and isolated in ghettos. The Amsterdam ghetto was even fenced in for a while, but it was later taken down. When the fencing was gone, signs saying "Jewish Neighborhood" remained. Olivia and the girls lived around the corner on the edge of that ghetto.

After being stripped of their rights, their jobs and income were taken away. They had to suffice with a minimum allowance and get food stamps for the basic staples needed to survive. That is when Hetty and her cousin Richy had lost their jobs. Their boss was no longer allowed to hire Jews. Perhaps the worst of it was that there was no opportunity for escape. The Jewish people had become unemployed, impoverished, and trapped. Only a few retained their jobs; luckily Sally had, and Fritz had, too. Fritz's income dwindled from a managerial salary down to only a small stipend, which was barely enough to survive on.

This stripping of rights went on until all registered Jews had been isolated and deported. By fall 1943, nearly all Dutch Jews had been put on transport and the community was erased.

11

HETTY, JUNE 1944

DAY FOUR AT AUSCHWITZ

On Hetty's fourth day at Auschwitz, something amazing happened. Someone from Hetty's past had spotted her.

Hetty had recognized Anna Rosenthal earlier, but she had had no way of getting her attention. Anna was a nice German woman she had known in the Netherlands before the war. She was about Hetty's age and was studying to be a nurse when they first met. Anna was blonde, beautiful, and elegant, and looked a great deal more German than Jewish and not as skinny as the rest. Her uniform was clean, and her hair had not been shaven off. She had long, cared-for hair and seemed to move freely around the camp.

When Anna found an opportunity to speak with Hetty, she told her that there was food in the kitchen that Anna had access to. She wanted to help Hetty because she thought Hetty looked weak, defeated and ill. This conversation took place when they were relatively alone and out of the direct sight of watchful eyes. Anna furtively handed her something to eat and warned Hetty about some of the atrocities taking place in Auschwitz.

"There is so much distress here, and I am at wits' end," she said.

She told Hetty that most people regarded her as a traitor because she wore eye make-up and still had her hair, clean clothes, and that she appeared healthier than the rest. Because no one else had access to make-up of any kind, everyone assumed she was sleeping with the enemy and couldn't be trusted. But she had done her best to help the sick whenever she could, and she promised to do the same for Hetty. She then told Hetty her own amazing story.

Anna had arrived at Auschwitz on a transport with more than 2,000 Jews. She was the only one still living from that group. It had been a dreadful realization, and she had been devastated. Things, however, had improved, perhaps because of her appearance. She had witnessed the rest going to the gas chambers. But the Nazis had selected her to work within the camp. One day, a German officer had taken a fancy to her, and she was forced to become his lover. Because of this special arrangement and due to her nursing experience, she was assigned to care for the sex slaves in the brothel. She was repulsed by the extent of sex crimes and the perverted abuse within the brothel. She had felt purpose when she brought extra food and care to those abused young women. Her lover was good to her, and she was grateful. Since resisting him might mean death she accepted his attentions and gifts, such as make-up, even though she received so much criticism for it. Wearing eye make-up was indeed a façade. She wore it as an overt thank you to her Nazi friend and to illustrate that she was loyal. The soldiers all knew that Anna would not be treated well by the inmates, and that suited them just fine. Anna fooled them into thinking that she was on their side and that they could trust her. It was at great risk for herself to play this game of charades with the Nazi officers.

Hetty wanted to relay the story of the young Kapo who had told the Philips group about the abuse that she and her brother had suffered but was careful not to say too much. Anna confirmed that there were "selections" performed especially for work in brothels. Young girls and boys were stolen from barracks in the middle of the night and were never seen again. They underwent regular sexual abuse by officers in Hitler's military. These children were all alone and held captive in the quarters of commanders who wanted to keep their pedophile behavior hidden.

In the brothel where Anna had worked in Auschwitz, children from 12 years old to young adult women of 22 were forced to accommodate the soldiers and Kapos. Each evening from eight to ten o'clock, and on Sunday afternoons, every 15 minutes another man entered and raped a girl, and in some cases, boys. Kindness and love were not permitted, and to prevent it there was a peephole into each room where the couples were being monitored while they fornicated. It was permitted to take out aggression and frustration on the girls. The women were selected for the men based on their looks and background. Slavic men could only see Slavic women, German men could only be with German women, etc. In order to avoid relationships forming, girls were never in the same room twice, and they were under lock and key at all other times. The program was a success for the Nazi military men, but less so for the prison inmates. The Nazis wanted to encourage them to work harder by promising they could climax with a live woman. Those prisoners performing slave labor who could get a woman for two Reichsmarks (less than $1) only wanted to use their time to talk with or be held by a woman.

Lena Smit had been separated from her daughter Lisabelle and was absolutely frantic, more so because Lisabelle was not well. There was nothing Hetty or anyone else could do about it. Lisabelle's condition was worsening to the point that she might need to go to the infirmary. She was all alone in sleeping barracks with strangers. She and Hetty did not know how to get a message to her, so Hetty thought up a plan to ask Anna for help. The idea that Lena might be forced to leave her daughter behind if she were moved elsewhere was such a heavy burden to her heart that it was tearing Lena apart.

Anna continued to help Hetty, searching for her a second and third time that day to give her some extra food. Hetty could tell by the way

Anna looked at her that she did not think that Hetty was going to make it. Given Anna's kindness to her, when she was able, she found a moment to ask Anna if she would mind if Lena Smit spoke with her in private regarding Lisabelle.

When the guards' attention was elsewhere, Lena approached Anna and whispered to her, "I see your make-up and know that other women here think you are a whore, sleeping with the Nazis for personal favors; but I know better." Lena looked around once again to be sure they could not be overheard. "I believe you are using your position to help other prisoners. Can I ask you one big favor? My daughter and I have been separated in the barracks. Can you get this message to her? She handed her a rolled up note to give to Lisabelle. If I am forced to leave my 14-year-old daughter behind in this place, and I am fearful that may happen, then there is no one to watch over her any more. I am pleading with you to do something for me. Please protect her and see to it that Lisabelle leaves here in one piece. Please don't let her die here all by herself, I beg of you, please? I will forever be indebted to you."

None of the women believed or expected that Anna could do anything to help Lisabelle survive. The inmates did not trust anybody who was sleeping with the enemy and were quick to judge Anna. But Lena had decided to believe in her. Anna gave Hetty and Lena her word, promising to help Lisabelle as best she could. Anna told them, "You have my word. I will do everything within my power to get Lisabelle away from here, alive and well."

12

FRITZ, JUNE 1945

THE NEW AMSTERDAM

Fritz was looking all around him and seeing things in a different way. Was this culture shock? Is this what happens when you are away from civilization for so long?

Fritz and Hetty had agreed on two things early on. First, if they were somehow separated along the way or were unable to find their way back to Amsterdam after the war, they had agreed that the Van Dyke home would be the first place each of them would try to reconnect.

Second, and the main agreement they had made, was to promise to stay alive. This promise between them was the driving force bringing him to the Van Dykes' doorstep today. He had lost track of Hetty's whereabouts for more than a year now but had never lost faith in her lust for life. He wanted to assume she was well and also on her way home.

The Dutch were known for their tolerance and open-mindedness. The Netherlands is a small country and has always been a melting pot of cultures. Before the war, Jews were treated well in the Netherlands, just like everyone else. They thought of themselves as Dutch citizens – and not as a religious group or a separate race. The

Dutch were the first European community that allowed people of all faiths to worship as they pleased – in the 16th century – under the Union of Utrecht.

Since the Nazi takeover, however, all Jews were in shock about being singled out and accused of being the villain. They had been falsely blamed for acts that had not been committed. No distinction had ever been made between people of different religions in over 400 years in the Netherlands. This was paramount.

The newly installed government, however, with its many new restrictions that had been enforced during the war, created a new and very deep divide in a country that had not known a racial divide for centuries.

Fritz had needed to concentrate on staying alive in the camps because everything, including the forced labor, was dangerous. He would often silently chant the mantra: pay attention, stay alert. Besides, he was not able to think straight back then. That is, he could not think things through because of sleep deprivation, malnutrition, and the constant mistreatment he had to endure. His mind could not come up with solutions to the problems he faced, and his mind and body had become numb to a number of emotions because of the need to survive. He made himself focus on the here and now. He encountered life-threatening situations on a daily basis, and ultimately, he concluded that the accumulated effects of starvation and dehumanization could destroy anyone.

But now he was able to think clearly again. There was so much for Fritz to contemplate and be grateful for. He had had the help of the Resistance during the war, which was composed of various cells throughout the Netherlands. The Resistance acted in secret and was actively opposed to Nazi rule, and Fritz had been associated with them before his deportation. They helped Jews go into hiding, or they could arrange for forged documents and offer to help Jews leave the country. It was a top-secret underground faction, and they had helped Fritz more than once. No one knew who the members were, which was for everyone's protection. Everything Fritz heard was on a need-to-know basis. The Resistance movement in Amsterdam had a hidden printing press and a secret team of dedicated volunteers who took personal risks to deliver and distribute forbidden news pamphlets and underground newspapers to all regions of the occupied territory. Possessing a radio, much less a printing press, had become a national offense punishable at the discretion of the Nazis during the war. The Resistance had managed to score a few radios and printing presses, and the news they heard on the British radio contradicted what the Germans were spreading about the state of the war. Statistics were made to be misleading, too, and the Nazis' many lies indicated that the Resistance had been eliminated, but the opposite was true.

The home of the Van Dykes signified the starting point of a second chance at life for Fritz. He had not yet ventured beyond this thought. For him, the future was entwined with Hetty, and his mind had no room for an alternative reality. He could not fathom life without her. No other future was even possible for him. He would not even consider that she was dead. He knew that this could be a foolish denial of the most probable outcome, yet Fritz would dismiss his fear before dismissing his hope.

His mind also occasionally dwelled on the other question that kept haunting him. "If I have lost all my loved ones, then what next? What is to become of me in such a world? I would just wither away from utter despair. Yet, having come this far, I can't give up. Things will work for me out somehow."

Since some people had managed to overcome despair like he had, there was enough resilience and hope to fall back on. Reviving hope, time and again, was a necessity. That was Fritz's experience in this war. Life had been dismantled against a backdrop of hatred. It had rendered synagogues barren of its members, the buildings left hollow and devoid of song. No one knew how they might emerge after this war because entire congregations had vanished. Would the Jews still believe in God, after this? Being on the receiving end of betrayal was brutal. It was like a contagious disease.

While imprisoned, the need to stay calm was paramount. "Keep to yourself, stay out of sight, be small, blend in, draw no attention to yourself. Do not protest, and let the insults just wash over you." That was another mantra of prisoners like Fritz. He had spent years dealing with constant brutality. By the end of the war, he was convinced that he had not seen the last of the prejudice against Jews. Fritz was so thankful that the war had lasted only five years. Imagine if the world had not responded to the plight of those who had suffered under diabolic treatment yet had managed to survive it? What if the Allies had not freed the camps? Or if they had not joined the combat and stepped into the war to overtake Hitler and his military?

Hitler and his generals had torn democracy apart. He was secretly in the mindset to become the dictator of Europe, and then of the entire world.

The possessions and property of the displaced Jews had been divided up among the Nazi elite only a few days following the eviction of each Jewish family. Envious of what the Jews possessed, the Nazis had put a lot of thought into stealing from them. Was it over? Could Fritz be confident that his possessions would be returned to him? These thoughts were interrupted by the sound of a familiar song. Fritz heard people singing. His companions on the flatbed began greeting people on the sidewalks, waving and smiling. There was recognition, laughter, and the men began singing the National Anthem together. Fritz looked up, letting his troubling thoughts go, and joined in the spontaneous merriment.

For a while he let his tears flow as a stream of people along the route spontaneously saluted him, bowed and waved. This was the answer to all his doubts – from now on, everything would work out.

Fritz reminded himself that the Nazis ruined their own economy, betrayed their own countrymen, sabotaged their enemies, and disgraced Germany. "Never forget that the German Nazis lost the war," Fritz's inner voice reminded him.

13

HETTY, JUNE 1944

THE LAST SELECTION

On the way to morning roll call, Hetty saw piles of corpses everywhere. It was horrifying. No one could tell whether there might be some people still alive in those piles. It was surreal – a real-life nightmare to see masses of skin and bones haphazardly lying about and rotting everywhere. The vile stench permeated everything, and other people were falling like flies.

The women prisoners already living in the barracks had told the Philips group that the murders had been scaled up at Auschwitz. In the course of a few months, the killing capacity had risen from 6,000 to 10,000 people per day. Jewish prisoners were gassed and burned on a daily basis, and the teeth of all prisoners with gold fillings or caps were extracted from the corpses before they were cremated or tossed into mass graves.

Most bodies were moved directly to the ovens and cremated, but when the executions were ramped up, even the many ovens couldn't handle the volume of prisoners murdered each day. And there weren't enough mass graves to deposit them in. It was evident that once they started using the gas chambers for killing around the clock, every day and night, the crematorium could not process so many corpses. Plus, the mass graves were simply not big enough nor could the digging of new ones keep up with the number of bodies needing to be processed. That is why so many people were lying around in decay.

It would later become known that the Nazi generals and several commanders of the extermination camps had held a special meeting to discuss how the pace of deposing of the bodies would be achieved. This was the Wannsee Conference, at which they designed what they called the "Final Solution to the Jewish Problem". But that was not all. There was a calculated and conscious decision made to speed up evacuations from transit and work camps and increase the processing of large numbers of corpses to get rid of what they termed "useless freight."

The Nazis trained their soldiers to abuse and terrorize those they deemed unworthy on a continual basis. Hetty had witnessed the temper tantrums, shouting, and verbal abuse for two years on the streets of Amsterdam before her capture. Spies lurked everywhere, and trusting strangers was impossible. During the year that she and others were imprisoned in Camp Vught, fellow inmates spied on them. She was watched during the day in the workplace, during roll call, in the lavatories, and at night in the barracks by the Kapos. She had come to know a few Kapos in Vught who spied on others in trade for food or a privilege of some kind. Even in Camp Vught, a bounty was awarded to collaborators who helped turn in prisoners who disobeyed the Nazi rules. She could only assume that the same system of spying was going on Auschwitz too.

Although Hetty was not detached from what was going on around her, many other Philips women were unable to comprehend their surroundings at all. In Auschwitz everyone looked sedated and in shock. They were barely present, seemingly in silent protest, with a dazed look in their eyes. They had apparently seen and smelled enough and had just disassociated from the world. Many had given up and found freedom in death.

Hetty was to turn 24 years old in July 1944. This was in just a few weeks. Hetty was not yet ready to die. She had more stamina than some of the older women. Although she understood how they felt, she had made an oath to stay sharp and do what was necessary to avoid death. Being observant and obedient was paramount, and she understood that any misstep at all was punishable by death in this place. But she vowed never to forget the promise she had made to Fritz to stay alive.

Hetty had no idea how hard it would be to survive the inhumanity that seemed to be everywhere. It was as if a contagious, murderous spell had been cast upon the entire population to become the cruelest version of themselves. It was as if they had all eaten from forbidden fruit and were addicted to aggression and had an undying thirst for unleashing more and more abuse. Where had humanity and decency gone? She refrained from thinking too long and hard about it, because she had no idea how bad it might get. She could not comprehend that things could get worse than this. She watched how the dehumanization here was killing many of her fellow workers. After all those days of misery and hunger, they were wasting away and barely alive.

Hetty dreaded what was to come here in this lost universe. The implication of what the guards had said about their loved ones all being dead was mortifying. She looked up to see the chimney towers filled with flames as the horrific fumes grew stronger. Were all of these flames the remains of her fellow workers? Her mind raced. She was very worried about Fritz, always conjuring up his face and keeping him alive in her heart and mind.

But where could he be? She had never stopped worrying about him. She tried to rid her mind of such uncomfortable questions so that nothing could cloud her judgment. Hetty whispered to strangers whenever the opportunity arose, asking if anyone had ever met Fritz Frankel, the furrier who worked for the De Klein clothing company in Amsterdam before the war. No one had.

The weather added to her torment because it was continually raining. Nothing protected any of them from the elements. Even in June. The only thing that had improved was the temperature, which was welcome, because they had slept in wet clothing last night. That night was unlike any Hetty had ever experienced in her life. Women had been shouting in a multitude of languages due to a variety of disputes, and were then beaten with sticks by the guards until the screams became sobs.

That young Kapo in the barracks may have looked small and frail, but she was in fact extremely cruel. She seemed programmed to do anything her superiors wanted. She had told Hetty and the women from the Philips group, "You're lucky if you get a tattoo with a number, because then you can leave here and go elsewhere and be put to work. That's not fair – you don't deserve it. You just got here."

The next day after roll call, Hetty's group was required to go to a building called the Sauna. The women were ordered to walk past a panel of Nazi judges. As always, these men were in their pressed uniforms, with hats cocked sideways, some with cigarettes hanging from their lips, others grinning, laughing, and ridiculing the women. Women guards stood nearby watching every move the prisoners made. As the women walked by, the judges examined them closely. Hetty had heard that sagging skin was a reason to be put to death. Those with bloated stomachs were ordered to go stand in the back of the room. Taking a quick glance at the back of the room, Hetty did not like what she saw.

The people there were the walking dead and looked like they had already given up the fight to survive. They looked hollow, as if there was no thinking mechanism inside; at least if there was, it was inactive. She knew that this group of people would likely be disposed of like trash. These zombies seemed to know what the verdict of this selection was going to be for them. Having been selected for execution, they were complacent and had acquiesced. This was not where she belonged.

Who they were, where they came from, or how old they were was impossible for Hetty to judge. All looked emaciated, old, and near death. Their bodies responded like robots, moving automatically and meekly obeying orders. Hetty surmised that these people were older than she was. But who could tell? They were probably going to die that day. This was a bad omen she couldn't accept.

Those selected for work or heavy labor were being sent to the front of the room. That much was certain. Hetty realized there were only two choices with essentially the same result: life imprisonment until death, or immediate execution. The stench of burning flesh coated her nostrils, and she nearly vomited.

When Hetty passed the judges, they had barely glanced at her. She was sent to the back of the room anyway. There she stood next to emaciated people with thermometers in their mouths. Then, someone with rough hands shoved a thermometer in her mouth. Minutes passed and she stood scanning the room. She saw people on the left side of the room standing in line for what looked like a painful procedure. Then another rough hand pulled the thermometer out of her mouth. She had a high fever. All the blood drained from her head. She was still not thoroughly recovered from the scarlet fever and stood trembling. Anticipating her next move, she considered going back to the judges again to show them her backside. In that oversized dress no one could see that she had firm buttocks. Flabby ones were a sign of malnutrition, and everyone knew it. Maybe this would save her. But her dress was so much larger than the petite body underneath. Her mind was racing trying to process the fact that she was being discarded and death was imminent.

She had to do something. But what? She surveyed the room again searching for a way out of this dilemma. The room was divided into rows of five, separated by ropes. Hetty noticed that those people on the far left were getting numbers tattooed onto their arms. "I must make sure that I get over there, to that row on the left," she thought. "That is where people are not being put to death, probably getting permanent numbers tattooed onto their arms. That means they have a future of some sort."

Just then, there was a sudden commotion on the far-right side of the room, and everyone turned to see what was going on. In that instant, Hetty saw her opportunity. Just before pulling up a rope to dive underneath, and move, she thought, "I can only die once. If they catch me, I'll be shot on the spot. But if I don't move now, I'll never see Fritz again and I'll never have children."

She seized the moment, that last thought propelling her forward. She took her chance to get where she needed to be. But there was a problem. She did not make it all the way over to the intended row in time before the guards turned back to watch the prisoners. As the commotion died down, Hetty found herself at an awkward distance between the row she had just left and the row she needed to be in. When a female Kapo standing nearby turned her attention to where Hetty stood, she screamed obscenities at Hetty and started beating her with a stick, pushing her over to the exact spot she needed to be. Hetty froze, now that she was in the proper row, obediently waiting in that line for a number.

Hetty's left arm was tattooed with the number 78323. She had become a number and would remain a number, no more than that. She had been branded like livestock, which was what she was to the Nazis. After receiving her number, she was ushered out of the Sauna. Just as she was approaching the exit, she looked back over her shoulder at the poor, impoverished people she had just stood beside only moments before. She could see despair in their expressions and saw their fate. The same fate that was also meant for her that she had somehow managed to evade.

One man in the back with cavernous, deep-set eyes looked directly at her. He silently mouthed, "I saw what you did," but he did not speak up and said nothing to anyone. No one betrayed Hetty. She held her stinging arm and let the drops of blood fall onto the ground as she said her goodbye to the one who let her go and thanked the lucky stars for having outsmarted her captors. She was able to return to the barracks and join the remaining women of the Philips group. It had worked. She was alive. She had defied the enemy – again!

Once she had a moment alone to reflect, she amazed herself that she had been able to trick the Nazis. Hetty was not a particularly brave person and did not ordinarily take risks. However, the risk she had just taken was far greater than an act of deception. It was Hetty, the warrior, taking charge of her own life. It was pure bravery. It was a game changer for her. The following day, she found out that she had been one of the lucky ones who was chosen to leave Auschwitz by train with the rest of the 250 women of the Philips group, who were being sent on to the next camp. The remaining 150 women they had been forced to leave behind in Auschwitz would not survive the war.

14

FRITZ, JUNE 3, 1945

ANYBODY HOME?

As the truck stopped at a square in the southern part of Amsterdam to let one of his travel buddies off, Fritz could hardly believe he was finally returning. It was a dream come true. Had everything changed or was it Fritz who had changed? Being free took some getting used to, but the joy hovering at the edges of his heart brought out the best in him. As he looked around at the scenery and buildings, he saw beauty all around. He remembered the culture and the freedom he had so loved in this wonderful city, and he reminded himself that it would be there again for him now. He would mend. He would live in this picturesque and heartwarming place and rebuild his life. Joy overcame him and he gladly let his thoughts wander back to that moment in time when his heart had been filled with love for a woman.

He could see Hetty in front of him. She was a bit of a coquette, which he loved. Like when she put her fingers over her mouth to hide her amusement. That never did work because her beautiful blue eyes lit up like candles. Her laughter seemed more prominent in his mind than most things about her, because it came from a deep place. It was a sound that he had never forgotten, one that was filled joy. It was one of the most appealing things about her. Fritz was suddenly overcome with these heartfelt memories and feelings of belonging.

Fritz slipped back to that exhilarating moment in spring 1942, when they had seen each other for the first time – it had been love at first sight. It was an afternoon in May, when the persecution of Jews was already well underway, but before the restrictions had become deadly. The weather had been glorious; the sun was shining, birds were chirping, with the light through the leaves scattered on the canals reminiscent of Renoir. Fritz loved to whistle to the birds, and that afternoon, alone in the splendor of a May day, he turned a corner and walked toward his apartment – the one he was sharing with his Uncle Benno.

Fritz had just been evicted, forced to move out of his spacious bachelor apartment on the Milletstraat. He would have been homeless were it not for Uncle Benno, who had offered to let Fritz stay with him at his apartment in the Jewish Quarter. Benno had also been forced to leave his home months before, downsizing to this small, one-bedroom apartment on the Lekstraat around the corner from the Van Dykes, whom he never had met. He had been used to a spacious apartment which he had been forced to relinquish, deed and all.

In the midst of whistling to the birds, Fritz stopped in his tracks, his whistle falling silent. He had spotted a beautiful woman sitting in a bay window on the second floor of an apartment just a short distance from his. As he stood looking up at her for a moment, she glanced up from her book, marked the page she was reading, and looked back down at him as he smiled up at her. Her wavy golden-brown hair made her appear angelic. Still smiling, he averted his eyes momentarily, only to look back in time to see her smile back at him. Something clicked inside of Fritz then. He recalled feeling shaky, as if he knew *This is the one.* The attraction was instant, compelling, and overpowering. He really wanted to meet this girl.

For the next week on his walk back from work, Fritz would look up to see her reading and would smile at her. It made the daily fears and Nazi occupation seem more distant for him, and he now looked forward to coming home each day. In an instant, he'd fallen in love. Everything else just receded into the background. It took only a few days of seeing each other in that manner to secure Fritz's affection for her. Each day they were on the lookout for one another, and Hetty obviously was waiting for him in the window when he returned home from work each day. It became clear that they were attracted to one another, and both seemed to sense when the other was nearing. Fritz's smiles would brighten her face, which made him even more eager to meet her. Fritz asked Benno if he knew the beauty down the street, always reading in the bay window. Benno knew Hetty's father and promised to introduce them.

When they were finally formally introduced, the chemistry was electric, even though Fritz was 14 years older than she was. The difference in age was immaterial to either of them. They had an instant connection unlike anything either of them had known before. Sparks flew. There was an undeniable energy in the air, and they were not shy at the meeting. The two had much in common. They had a similar background, both from educated, middle-class Jewish families. They were both non-observant Jews, and both had had a happy childhood. They generally felt secure and safe, with a bright future ahead of them. In addition, they both had an eye for fashion, Fritz designing and producing fur coats for a clothing firm in Amsterdam.

They were swept into a romantic whirlwind of laughter and chatter, sometimes drifting back and forth into a world without war. Being so attracted to one another in wartime heightened their senses and brought them closer, but it did not make them careless. The imminent possibility of danger permeated everything around them, and though they remained wary of the Nazi presence everywhere, they began to feel invincible, just as all young lovers do.

They tried to see each other as often as possible. More meetings followed rapidly, during which Fritz got to know Hetty's father, Martin, and the Van Dykes. Then, only two months later, after being tipped off by the Resistance group of a crucial meeting regarding the newest development in the Nazi mandates, Fritz had decided to marry Hetty at once.

The truck was at last standing in front of the Van Dyke's door in Amsterdam, the moment of truth having arrived. Fritz was pulled out of his reverie by the chauffeur, who saw that Fritz was deep in thought. "Where was she now?" Fritz wondered as he gazed toward the sky. The driver yelled something to Fritz that pulled him back into the present. He gathered his few belongings, waved goodbye to his travel companions, and hopped off the truck. Fritz had genuine butterflies in his stomach, terrified of what might happen next. He feared finding out what truth was lying behind that door. But he was destined and primed to find out. This longing had gone on long enough. He needed to see his wife. He wanted just to touch and hold her.

Fritz took a rag from his pocket and wiped his neck and forehead with it. He hoped to look presentable, though knew it was impossible. Rags were all he had been able to gather when he'd left the last concentration camp, where the uneventful liberation had finally come to pass. Rags would have to suffice for now. The temperature had made his soiled uniform stick to his back, and he did not want to see Hetty this way. But what choice did he have? He had no other clothes and only a few newly acquired items, like a comb and toothbrush, in his knapsack.

He suddenly felt frozen in the midday sun. He knew when he rang the doorbell that if the Van Dykes were at home and there was bad news about Hetty, his dreams would be shattered, his hopes over. He faced the building as if it were a firing squad. He approached the door and rang the bell.

It was about noon. A stormy mix of dread, worry, and hope flooded his entire being, and he felt as if his feet were nailed to the steps. He began frantically knocking on the door with one hand and yanking the doorbell pulley with the other. At the same time, he shouted, "Anybody home?" Aware of his messy appearance, he took a step back and looked up toward the second floor. He saw that a window was open. He then heard movement on the other side of the door and heard voices. Could it be true? Were they home? Would they all be at home now? Olivia, Fleur, Sally, and Hetty? He swallowed, took a deep breath, and felt his heart pounding in his chest. Would he be welcomed with warmth and recognition by friends, or would he be met by strangers with hostility? Would there be new people living here who would deny him entry and turn him away? People could be aggressive to anyone who tried reclaiming anything. But then he saw Fleur smiling down at him. It turned out that Fleur, Sally, and their mother, Olivia Van Dyke, were all at home that afternoon when Fritz arrived.

Fritz did not really believe he would find Hetty at the van Dyke home that afternoon. Even if they were at home, the idea that he would find his wife sitting there safe and sound waiting for him was too fantastic to be true. Yet, conjured images don't lie, and the more they are fed in The Memory Place, the greater the likelihood that they come true. They materialize, Fritz remembered. The picture-perfect image, the one of Fritz and Hetty wrapped around one another in a deep embrace, was at the forefront of his mind. He was sure that he would hold her in his arms once again.

He never for a moment assumed that she would not be ready to see him, that all these dreams would come crashing to an end, or that she might push him away because she was too hurt. Never did he for a moment entertain the idea that on the other side of the door, a crippled Hetty would reject him, too embarrassed to allow him to see what damage had been done by the monsters she had had to deal with in his absence. No, the image that he fostered was a loving, accepting one, and that would keep him going, no matter what.

When the doorbell rang, Fleur, then in her twenties, gazed out of the third story window and saw skinny Fritz standing on the stoop eagerly looking up toward her. Seeing him standing there, his cropped hair, his slight mustache, his worn and fragile appearance with that awful striped prison clothing, made her weak in the knees as she breathed a sigh of relief. There he was. Fritz. Back from the war, from the camps. Here. Free. His and Hetty's return was something she had prayed for every day but hadn't dared hope for. But here he was – back from the dead, it seemed. So many had not returned, their whereabouts unknown. Fleur knew about the fate of many who had viciously and mercilessly been murdered.

With great joy and seeing an anxious smile on Fritz's face, Fleur's eyes locked on his and she felt faint with delight. She would have recognized him anywhere. "*Fritz!*" she shouted.

Fleur watched as he descended the steps to gather his things, obviously alive and able to walk, although he seemed to have a slight limp and was in some pain. With a look of hopeful anticipation, he kept grinning at her. She quickly whirled about and ran as fast as she could down two flights of stairs, nearly tripping as she went. Her sister, Sally, emerged from another room and joined Fleur rapidly descending the stairs. Olivia arrived at the front door with her two daughters at exactly the same time.

As Fritz watched the door open, tears streamed down his face and he fell into the warm embrace of his good friends, these people he loved, the only people he was sure would welcome him with open arms, even in his present state. These were the people he could surrender to and grieve with. People who loved him. People whom he could trust. *Life will be better now*, was his first and only thought as he fell apart and loudly wept.

Map of Nazi-occupied territory in Europe

PART 2

WORLDS DISCONNECTED

15

HETTY, JUNE 1944

TRIALS AND TRIBULATIONS

Hetty could not sleep, in anxious anticipation of leaving Auschwitz for a new camp. Although sleep had abandoned her, she could not bear to be aware of her surroundings, because so many people all around her had become dangerous. She was scared, exhausted, and still recovering from her illness. Adrenaline had kept her awake. Also, aggressive inmates from other countries were shouting. The constant moaning and sobbing made sleep impossible.

She'd had stray visions of escaping, and focused on memories of Rosalie, her second mother. She remembered the first escape attempt she had made with Rosalie, just before the war broke out. Hetty knew exactly the person she would contact in the event she returned from the war, if she managed to survive. First and foremost, she would go to see the Van Dykes in Amsterdam. She hoped her father and Hans would be back there when she arrived; but if for some reason they were all nowhere to be found, she would locate Aunt Rosalie. Hetty was certain her aunt would still be alive, well, and safe in America. She had memorized the New York addresses of Aunt Rosalie and Rosalie's brother, Uncle Daniel.

Hetty was no longer the vivacious, carefree young girl she had been when Rosalie last saw her in 1940. Back then, she was mostly preoccupied with whether she might lose her job in the event of war. She was not yet concerned about losing her family or being killed. *How bad could it get?* she had wondered. Her thoughts were that of a 19-year-old, worrying only about girly things, like fashion and her appearance. She typically daydreamed about finding a boyfriend and flirted with the friends of her older brother, Hans. Hans had really cute friends, and although she had a crush on one of them, named Max, she had never really felt he was at all interested in her. She also had girlfriends whom she used to get together with to do makeovers when they were growing up. But the giggles and girly things they did seem to put Max off. He didn't have a sister, so he thought they were silly. Hetty decided Max was oblivious and stuck up.

She had spent most of her time at home reading magazines and books. An avid reader, she went to the library a few times a week. She could read quickly and enjoyed fantasizing while reading good stories, mostly with romance or adventure themes. She always took great care in planning her wardrobe and was an excellent seamstress. Most of what she wore she had made herself. She put lots of time and energy into what to wear to their Friday night family gatherings.

Hans was also living at home at the time, but he was very concerned about an impending war and was willing to fight against Germany if a war broke out. She had left any thinking about war to the men. It was not that she wasn't smart; she was always concerned with keeping up with the news. Hetty was interested to know what all the "fear and fuss," as she put it, was about. What potential schemes or strategies could the Nazis be concealing? She just felt that, being a girl, she would never have to be a soldier and go to battle. Little had she known that she ultimately would.

She did not really envision that anything truly terrible would happen – she had always been a trusting girl. Even at only 14, she had often biked home alone in the dark after going to the movies with friends.

Sometimes it would take an hour to reach the Van Dyke's home on the other side of the river IJ, but she was not concerned about being assaulted or of being by herself. Her youth had been basically peaceful, and the world was not very scary. At that time, the Van Dykes lived on the northern banks of the IJ river in pre-war Amsterdam.

No one knew at the beginning of the war what would happen to their carefree lives, but Hetty had already decided that she wanted to go to America and maybe one day become an actress or a designer. She was working for Paramount Pictures, translating scripts from English into Dutch, making subtitles along with her cousin, Richy, and drooling over the great Hollywood stars and starlets. She worked in the heart of Amsterdam, a short bike ride from home. She loved to read about the Dutch royal family and was always interested in their activities. When the war broke out, the Dutch Queen, Wilhelmina, fled to England, where she continued to carry out her duties from abroad. Hetty did not understand, thinking that the Queen was abandoning them. She became angry when the lives of so many Jews were threatened in her city.

Hetty could have been considered a bit of a charmer by her brother and father, because she knew how to get her way with them. She was the apple of her father's eye, especially since she had become the lady of the house when her mother, Bertie, passed away. It had been a difficult time, but Hetty figured it had been hardest on her father. In that regard, she could also be found play-acting her grief away and entertaining other members of the family with make-believe stories she had extracted from books. She loved the drama of Hollywood films and could re-enact scenes from movies. Too bad that Uncle Daniel lived on the East Coast of the US, because she had big plans for herself in Hollywood. She was a gifted designer and could mix and match and alter old outfits to make them stylish. She always looked fashionable and was not hindered by her small budget because she created long-lasting styles. Her reflection in the mirror pleased her because every style looked good on her petite feminine frame. She knew she would be good at stardom. However, if her American entertainment plans did not work out, she did have a Plan B. She loved knitting and designing knit dresses, and that vocation seemed like a good back-up if her plans for Hollywood fell through.

Uncle Daniel had sent Hetty an invitation to visit him in New York in summer 1939, but she did not have the money to do so; nor did she think it was a good idea to leave her father for so long. The crossing on an ocean liner would have cost too much, and she did not have the savings for such an expensive trip. Besides, the voyage to and from the United States was a long one, and although it would be fun, there would not be enough time to visit New York properly. Flying was out of the question. The common man could not afford it. Aunt Rosalie and Cousin Richy had lived there before and had always told such wonderful and glorious stories about the place. Their other relatives in New York were also enthusiastic about having her visit. Once, when the entire family was invited, her father shrugged his shoulders and said, "I might consider tagging along with this blossoming starlet."

Hetty knew for certain that she would be safe in America. Only European countries were being threatened by the growing tension and antisemitism that had been growing in Germany. More reason to leave. Their Dutch family had gathered around the radio and listened to Winston Churchill on the BBC when he warned listeners of an impending war. But no one in the Netherlands was worried much because the country had managed to stay neutral during World War I.

Although Uncle Daniel was Dutch, he had been living in New York for a few decades. After Rosalie had married and moved to Manhattan, Hetty's cousin Richy was born. Shortly thereafter, Rosalie's husband died of a sudden heart attack at a young age, which had motivated Rosalie and baby Richy to return to her Dutch family in Amsterdam. Richy had grown up next door and was like another brother to Hetty and Hans.

Before the war began, Rosalie and Richy both still had valid passports for the USA, which were soon set to expire. The two of them knew it was a good time to escape Amsterdam and return to New York for good. Although both Rosalie and Richy were frightened about staying in the Netherlands, they were also reluctant to leave. They discussed their dilemma privately with Martin, Hetty, and Hans. Might they be willing to risk an escape together as a family?

At the end of 1939, the five of them had agreed to make an attempt to escape. The war had just broken out in Europe in September, and the need to leave became obvious. Martin planned for them to escape to England. He was certain that the Jewish community in London would help them find refuge.

Martin and Rosalie had expended most of their savings to buy five tickets for the family to cross the English Channel aboard a cargo ship. They told no one. The freighter was to leave from the IJmuiden wharf at dawn. The five of them left Amsterdam for the coast of IJmuiden at night – on foot, with all their luggage, taking only the bare necessities, leaving everything else behind in their apartments. They walked for hours in the dark along the Hemweg to the waterfront, keeping mostly to the shadows. They arrived on time, without incident. There they waited at the appointed dock ... and waited ... and waited – but no ship ever came. There was no vessel nor other passengers on the dock. There was nothing else to see at this now-abandoned wharf. It had all been a wild goose chase. A lie. A con. A robbery.

Many other Jews had lost their savings in the exact same way. It was a tremendous disappointment for them all, and Hetty took it to heart. This was her first real experience of disappointment in mankind. A successful escape would have prevented all of their suffering. What could have been the beginning of a new adventure became a crushing disappointment for all of them.

Although Martin thought that he could trust the person from whom he had purchased the tickets, he had been swindled. He was devastated, and he had no savings left for a second chance. They all walked back to Amsterdam, forlorn. This deception had a major effect on them all. Hetty went from being a carefree young girl to becoming a cautious young adult at age 19. This thwarted escape attempt had killed her innocence. She was still cheerful, but it had made her wary of trusting anyone from then on. Since the betrayal, Hetty had become another person altogether.

After their unsuccessful escape, the family discussed their options, and they concluded that only Rosalie and Richy had any. The rest of them would have to wait it out in the Netherlands. Nobody could have envisioned the terror that was to come, losing everything, down to their skin, or losing their wives, lovers, mothers, fathers, brothers, sisters, children, infants, aunts, uncles, grandparents, pets, and friends.

Hetty and her father and brother did their best to convince Rosalie and Richy that they should try leaving again, because they had the passports to enter the US, where they would be permitted to stay and work. Now, in wartime, the stakes would be much higher. They did not want to leave Martin, Hetty, and Hans behind, but there were no other options. Rosalie had received word about a ship leaving for New York from Lisbon, which was about 2,000 kilometers away in Portugal. If their information was correct, this ship would be the last one permitted to take immigrants. It would be their only chance to leave the European continent. This escape attempt would be even riskier than before. Much riskier.

If Rosalie and Richy were stopped, questioned, and suspected of wrongdoing while underway to Lisbon, they would probably be killed by the Nazis or their sympathizers. That ship was scheduled to depart for the States in mid-July, and they needed time to get there. They needed to make haste if they wanted to make it. This time it was just the two of them leaving, and with the other failed escape attempt on their minds, they still were still reluctant to go. This time, they had hoped they would not have to rely on anyone else to make it all happen; however, they would need fake papers drawn up in a hurry.

Hetty had memorized Uncle Daniel's American phone number. Telephones were still relatively scarce in private households, and only businesses could afford them. But Uncle Daniel had an office in New York, and his Dutch relatives knew they could always count on Daniel's help.

Because Richy was born on American soil, he automatically had American citizenship; but his US passport was about to expire, and getting the required paperwork now was not as easy as before. The Nazis had taken control of City Hall and were determining who could leave the country. The borders had been closed to Jews. The government, now controlled by the Nazis, had restrictions for travel that pertained to all Dutch residents. This was an obstacle that Rosalie and Richy would need to overcome if they were to leave.

There were administrative delays with the paperwork, and they could not leave before permission was granted. So they went to a Resistance comrade whom Rosalie knew, Stan Davids, who was able to get them the forged documents in time.

Meanwhile, they had mapped out the route they would take. Only Hetty, Hans, and Martin knew of these plans. All their other relatives were told nothing, for everyone's safety. Hetty had not yet met Fritz at this point.

Not all of Rosalie and Hetty's family in Amsterdam participated in the Friday night gatherings on a regular basis anymore, but they all knew each other well. Everyone else was just afraid of losing their jobs and disobeying the newly imposed rules. A few relatives acted as though there was nothing urgent to get worked up about. Only Rosalie was willing to undertake such a lengthy and dangerous endeavor to leave the Netherlands. Rosalie was able to take shorthand in all of the five languages she spoke fluently, having had years of experience working as a private secretary in the US. Therefore, she was confident that she would find good-paying work there, or in any country of her choosing. That confidence gave her the courage to fool the Nazis.

Rosalie and Richy would need to succeed in getting past all the border patrols enroute through occupied Belgium, warring France, and Franco's Spain in order to board a ship from Lisbon to freedom. With Hitler's Italian fascist friend Benito Mussolini at the helm in Italy, there was increased tension there. With the formation of the Axis powers who partnered with Germany now gaining strength in Europe, Rosalie and Richy anticipated a scary journey, knowing that each time they showed their identity papers, they would be tempting fate.

They also knew that the Nazis had annexed Austria in 1938, followed by Czechoslovakia and Hungary. The Netherlands and Poland had capitulated. Spain was willing to make a deal with Germany for its sovereignty, and France was currently at war with Germany for control. That meant the enemy would be all around them as they traveled.

From left to right: Hans, Rosalie, Daniel, Hetty, and Bertie

16

FRITZ, JUNE 1945

TIME FOR FREEDOM

Once inside the Van Dyke home, Fritz was practically carried into the living room and encouraged to rest. Despite his aches and pains, he was full of joy and had a multitude of questions. Olivia, now 60, took charge. She offered Fritz food and drink while the sisters kept touching him as proof of life. They were like hens pecking at him, asking permission to rub his back and to comfort him in any way. He did not smell bad, but his prison uniform, besides being offensive, was terribly soiled and ragged. The girls flooded him with warmth and affection. Everyone's cheeks were wet with tears, and they couldn't stop smiling.

Fritz knew the apartment well, although most of the wooden furniture he remembered was gone. He kept questioning them with his eyes, but for some reason, when he wanted to ask about Hetty his courage abandoned him. He turned his attention to the women in those first few minutes and tried to acclimate to his new situation.

He was brought a sandwich and a glass of milk, and he ate everything eagerly amidst the chattering of the three women, who babbled on about how they had gone searching for him and Hetty after their disappearance. They told him that the whole neighborhood had been emptied shortly after Fritz and Hetty had disappeared. Olivia and her daughters were the only ones left on their street. The Nazis had barricaded every street and emptied them one by one, taking hundreds of families per day and sealing each home. Within hours, truckloads of valuable art, jewelry, and heirlooms were taken from these apartments. The population of the entire Jewish ghetto had been seized and deported.

After some moments, Olivia took Fritz upstairs to the sober-looking, nearly bare, attic room that housed a freshly made-up bed seemingly awaiting him as if he had been expected to arrive that very day. Besides this, there was a writing table upon which a small radio and a wind-up clock stood perched as if time had stood still. The ladies carried his sparse belongings upstairs while he hashed over in his mind what they had told him when he'd finally been able to ask about Hetty and her family.

Unfortunately, the Van Dykes had heard nothing about Hetty's brother and father, Hans and Martin Golden. They had heard about what became of Uncle Benno, though, and this was sad news indeed. Benno had apparently committed suicide the same day that Fritz and Hetty had secretly wed. He had jumped into the canal and drowned, consciously intending to end his own life. At the time, everyone had blamed Benno's disappearance on the Nazis, and Benno likely thought it was better that way; probably the reason why he left no note. Fritz would not have to feel any blame. Benno probably did not want to tell anyone of his plan, least of all Fritz, so as not to ruin his wedding day. It was only later that someone had found Benno's body in the canal.

It took a while for Fritz to absorb the news. It was horrible and painful, but also understandable. Fritz could identify with wanting to commit suicide as a way to escape, because he himself had wanted to do so more than once in the last few years. Fritz remembered Benno discussing the possibility of suicide once before, when they first started living together in 1942, after Fritz had been evicted from his own bachelor apartment. Apparently, Benno had been giving it more thought than Fritz had realized. After hearing from Fritz what the Resistance members had told him about upcoming deportations, with extermination camps built in the East for eliminating Jews, Benno had made up his mind to commit suicide. He had quickly realized that deportation meant death.

Fritz told the women what he knew about Uncle Benno, and that Benno had lost hope in mankind by then. His uncle had always said that he would decide his own fate. He never intended to go on transport when summoned, or to suffer at the hands of the enemy. Perhaps, Fritz thought, the wedding might have hastened Benno's plan. Knowing that Hetty and Fritz had each other to rely on meant that he could now leave, and the married couple could have the apartment to themselves. Fritz realized that Benno had been very selfless that day, though the pain of missing him would linger forever.

Then, there was Hetty. The only thing that Olivia could confirm for certain about Hetty was that, a year ago, three days before D-day, Hetty had written a very short note that had been tossed out of a cattle car she was in. The train had been stopped at a busy station somewhere near the border with Germany. A Dutch woman passerby had noticed a hand tossing the paper out of one of the air vents in a cattle car, and she saw where it had landed on the tracks. The woman looked all around to see whether anyone else had noticed, or was watching her, and no one was. She had climbed down onto the tracks and retrieved the little folded note. This kind stranger sensed the urgency of what the note said and mailed it to Olivia in Amsterdam. It read, "We are leaving Camp Vught. Destination unknown. Hetty." It was dated June 3, 1944, addressed to Olivia. The very last news anyone had heard from Hetty was a year ago today.

"Oh no!" Fritz gasped. "A whole year. Anything could have happened!"

What had become of her? His stomach clenched with fear and anxiety. He was suddenly frozen with terror. If her train had left just a few days before the Allied forces landed, she would have arrived at a concentration camp on D-day, and anything could have happened to her after that. Although the coastal invasion of France by the Allies had changed the course of the war, it took eleven more months for the war to officially end. However, Fritz had heard that Auschwitz, the main extermination camp, was liberated by the Russians coming from the East on January 27, 1945. Still, it would be very difficult to trace her steps from a cattle car on its way to anywhere.

"Oh no, no, no," he kept saying. It was all that Fritz could utter. He slowly put his face in his hands and shook his head silently as his eyes filled again with tears. His grief was overwhelming; he was having trouble breathing.

The women looked on in silence, grieving with him, yet allowing Fritz his moment of despair. What else could they do?

Even though the Allies had made it through the front lines, the war did not end soon after D-Day. Progress was slow, but steady, the Allied forces freeing cities in France one by one, as they headed northeast. That unfortunately gave the Nazis eleven more months of killing civilians. There were many battles and setbacks on both sides, with Allied troops bound together to defeat Hitler. *Ultimately, the allies won,* thought Fritz, but not before the Nazis would send hundreds of thousands more souls to their deaths in the last throes of the war.

Fritz was silent for a while, thinking about what he knew of the rescue mission. He knew that the Allies had suffered great losses, but they had also succeeded in getting behind enemy lines. The Russian Red Army had freed Fritz from Schindler's Brünnlitz concentration camp, but they had not done so until May. If Hetty had lived and been freed by the Red Army in January, she should have been home by now. Most other camps farther east were still functioning right up until the final days of the war, which ended only after Hitler and his generals committed suicide in a bunker in Berlin. Only then, on May 8, 1945, with the demise of Hitler and the Third Reich, was World War II officially declared over. *So much could have happened to her*, Fritz kept thinking – and he was closer to the truth than he knew.

Fritz told the women what had happened to him and Hetty, how they had been abducted in the middle of the night and sent to Camp Vught. The last he had known of Hetty was when he was sent away to Auschwitz by train. She had stayed behind and was, as far as Fritz knew, still held captive in the women's camp there, probably still working at Escotex.

He told them how he and a group of more than 300 men and boys had suddenly been evacuated from Camp Vught. The journey was long and terrible, and the destination unspeakable. They had been sent first to Westerbork and then directly on to Auschwitz. He had never encountered anything so dark and sinister as that Polish camp, Auschwitz, which reeked of death. It had been sheer hell. He shuddered now at the thought that Hetty may have been there as well. She could easily have been extinguished there like so many others had been.

He looked up at the women. Besides having questions for these women, he needed to tell them what it was like living in Camp Vught so that he could compare the two. He did not know where to begin. But he thought he would start at the beginning.

"We were at Camp Vught together for ten months after leaving Amsterdam," Fritz told the women. "The men and women were separated and kept in different areas in different barracks, according to gender, nationality, age, and profession. We had never expected that. But it got so much worse and so unbearable, truly unimaginable.

I was devastated at not being able to say goodbye to her. After we left, there was no way of knowing anything about her at all."

He told them about Vught's deplorable conditions. It had been built in May 1942 and consisted of 36 living barracks and another 23 buildings where work was performed. Two rows of high-voltage barbed-wire fencing almost 4 meters tall surrounded the camp, and armed guards were stationed in watchtowers around the perimeter. The SS officers ran the place with an iron fist, and they had their own quarters outside the camp border. The first prisoners had arrived from another camp in Amersfoort; badly beaten, ill, and starving, they were marched from the train station to the camp, where they started work on the barracks. Many expired there.

"We hated it," he remembered. "The conditions were awful, like nothing we had ever imagined. We were expecting paying jobs, like they promised us. But the Nazis had betrayed our trust and had created a workforce consisting of slave laborers in a prison camp. Luckily, Hetty and I were able to see each other now and then because we both worked in a plant sewing for Escotex. We worked in the same sweatshop, which was a lucky break," he said.

"Seeing her every day made it all bearable somehow, even if we were not allowed to talk with one another. On the day we men had to leave the camp I couldn't reach her or get a message to her, and I was so upset."

The women were sitting in stunned silence, anticipating the rest of his story. They still couldn't believe that he was sitting there in front of them, alive.

"The trip to Auschwitz lasted four days and four nights under the worst of conditions. We had been beaten and thrown into an open cattle car, with no food or water, and there was no toilet, just a pail. Some did not even survive the transport in that filthy, vile freight car."

As he spoke, his eyes remained mostly on the floor, only occasionally looking up. He paused often to gather his emotions.

"When everyone started disappearing from Amsterdam it was bad enough, as you know. No idea where everyone had been taken. But we couldn't have ever imagined the truth at the time. Nor could we imagine what lay ahead. While we were in Vught we constantly looked for our families and asked whether anyone had seen them, but we found no one. Vught was so big – maybe 10,000 people were there when we arrived. We were very worried, but we had the illusion that, somehow, we would meet Martin and Hans and the others in that camp. We had no idea what really went on or if there were more camps like this. Did you know that there were hundreds of work camps and many death camps, hidden away in remote areas in the East? Working at Vught was nothing like the propaganda films we had seen making the camps look attractive."

At that moment, Fritz realized that what had happened to him was not his fault. They had been fooled by well-crafted propaganda into believing the Nazis' promises. But they had all been deceived.

"We had no idea how bad the transports would be or that we would be human freight, intentionally made to suffer. The Nazis' shouting never stopped. Cruelty was an effective weapon used to demoralize us and wear us down over time. They crammed many more people into the cattle cars than could comfortably fit. Some not only fainted but were trampled and suffocated to death. We had not imagined that almost all of our belongings would be stolen from us immediately. We could not understand or imagine what a death camp would look like or how it worked. Why kill us? Who would do that? We were productive members of a growing society. But we found ourselves in the middle of a well thought-out and planned ethnic program to eliminate us. We were the target of a catastrophic genocide."

17

HETTY, JUNE 1944

ESCAPE

Hetty tried to conjure up the faces of loved ones as she lay uneasily in the bunk with the other women on her last night in Auschwitz. She could easily recall how all three Goldens had prayed that Rosalie and Richy would succeed in their escape.

Hetty had been particularly sad about their leaving. Richy had been her buddy at work, and he would be terribly missed. She was also aware that when she went to work, she would be asked about his sudden disappearance and ongoing absence, and she had to come up with a story to offer when she was questioned. She prepared a script and practiced it, as an actress would. She rehearsed what she was going to tell her boss – or anyone else who asked about Richy or Rosalie's whereabouts.

On Rosalie and Richy's departure day in July 1940, Hetty, then 20 years old, and Hans, 21, escorted their aunt and cousin by train as far as the Dutch-Belgian border, where they parted ways. Hetty and Hans gave their aunt and cousin a big hug and stepped off the train. They all knew it was unlikely that they would see one another ever again. As the whistle blew and the train stated to move, they stood waving goodbye until it was totally out of view.

From the border with Belgium, Rosalie and Richy's journey took them across many guarded borders and through the cities of other occupied countries. Mother and son needed to make haste if they were to arrive in Lisbon on time. They only had a few weeks to get there and no means other than trains. They had calculated that the transatlantic ocean liner voyage from Lisbon to New York would take about nine days; Rosalie and Richy hoped to arrive in New York by early September 1940. The trip would cost the Levys their entire savings.

Half of their family gone, Hetty and Hans viewed each other differently now. They were adults and had to face the war together. Now, they had only each other and their father, whom they vowed to care for. Hetty held her head high, and even though she was devastated, she tried to console herself knowing that her brother and father were nearby and would do their best to protect her always. She felt a sense of purpose by playing the actress she now needed to be. She wanted to go home and practice being someone else, someone more confident and determined. She would need to remain silent and listen carefully to what older adults were saying, because she heard dramatic stories about the war all around her. Remaining silent was not easy for her. She was always inclined to speak out at will; but she found comfort in knowing that her brother would have to do the same thing. Everyone who was being hunted down had had to reinvent themselves somewhat. She created a second personality in which emotion was concealed. Not easy, as she was such an emotional creature. She would need to keep many secrets to herself and maintain a façade for the outside world. But, inside, she was growing more and more frightened.

Hetty, Hans, and Martin spent an anxiety-ridden summer wondering about what could have gone wrong, but they finally received a joyous letter from Rosalie in fall 1940. She and Richy had arrived safely in

New York, where life was free of the worries of war. Rosalie said she followed the news closely, expecting the worst. She knew that the antisemitic sentiment in Europe had increased and needed to be taken seriously.

With a little help from her brother, Daniel, Rosalie had found work. Soon afterward, Richy did too, and in no time, Rosalie was back to living the life she had once known. It was all just like it should be for everyone, Rosalie wrote. They had all the conveniences and freedoms people should have, and life there was good.

Hetty believed that Rosalie and Richy had done the right thing by leaving, even if they missed each other every day. Hetty's letters from the Netherlands came frequently at first and sounded hopeful and informative. Uncle Daniel wrote to invite Hetty to come and stay again, but it was now definitely too late for any of them to leave. Later, when Hetty wrote to Rosalie, Richy, and Daniel about meeting Fritz and getting married, they were happy for her. Hetty didn't mention the Resistance or other things that needed to remain a secret from the Nazis. She was rightfully afraid that the mail might be intercepted and that she could put the family and others in harm's way. All mail was censored, so it was good that she was careful about what she wrote to them. Her writing began showing signs of real worry, though, and some of her former glow was missing.

In her letters, Hetty openly expressed her love for Fritz to Rosalie, but there was noticeably less optimism in them as time went on. Both the tone and the frequency of the letters lessened, Hetty sounding depressed and scared. Both she and Fritz had become fearful, and in June 1943, Hetty's letters to Rosalie ceased altogether. Rosalie had no idea that they had been captured by the Nazis.

18

FRITZ: JUNE 1945

CHILDREN SENT AWAY

Flashback to 1943

Fritz had so much to tell the Van Dykes; he was glad he was finally able to share his stories. The women were very grateful to hear things first-hand.

"A few days before we arrived at Camp Vught, something unimaginable had happened to the prisoners there. We were terrified when we heard about it, and shocked when we saw their anguished faces. Everyone was miserable and many were crying. Some committed suicide because of it."

Fritz explained, "All the children had been loaded onto railway cars and sent away, many completely on their own, crying and miserable. The parents and other relatives who were left behind were more than devastated. The suffering was palpable, but the Nazis still forced everyone to continue working. It was hard for anyone to concentrate, but those left behind were all expected to work as if nothing had happened. They were utterly depressed and desperate. Everyone in the barracks was in shock."

On June 6 and 7, 1943, two trains with almost 1,300 Jewish children were sent away from the camp. All children under 16 had to leave on this transport, parents accompanying the children aged three and younger the first day, with the rest of the children through age 16 sent away alone the next. They were told that they would be going to a special camp for children; but, in truth, the trains traveled first to the Westerbork transit camp and from there on to the Sobibor death camp in Poland. They were all murdered upon arrival.

Some who could work needed the distraction, but there was no mercy from the hateful guards when someone stopped working to wipe tears away or just pause for a moment. Then, the SS would intervene.

"No one yet knew what the fate of those young children and babies would be" Fritz told them. "There was no way to comfort the relatives who had been left behind. Hetty and I were just aghast at how everyone was being treated. But seeing the remaining parents of the deported children and hearing their stories of the brutality committed there; that was enough for us to panic.

"This knowledge made it even harder for us to acclimatize because we were traumatized within a day," Fritz continued. "When we arrived, all of our belongings were confiscated."

"We had no one familiar to talk to in our separate barracks. Everything was new, and it took quite some time to adjust to the aggressive treatment, the threats, the beatings, and the roll calls, and it was impossible to trust anyone after having been lied to so cruelly.

"But having your children taken like that – there are no words for doing something so sadistic. Everyone assumed the worst had happened to those children. It was only a while ago that I heard that the trainload of children and infants had perished. If they had survived, which we didn't believe, the littlest ones would not even have known their own last names," Fritz said. "They would have become lost orphans. How would they ever find their families again? It was heart-wrenching. It still is."

Fritz paused a while, and the women brought him more food and something to drink. They conferred with each other and asked him more questions about Camp Vught. "We found out that many different groups had been persecuted," he told them. "Rounded up and brought to this camp like we had been. Not only Jews, but also others – including students, hostages, political prisoners, Jehovah's Witnesses, black-market dealers, and the disabled. There were colored badges sewn onto our uniforms to create competition amongst us, because some groups received normal meals. We didn't. We started studying the colors and finding out which groups were spying on us. We could tell that no one in the barracks could be trusted either. We all received a tin cup for drinking and eating, and without it we would have starved. I was terrified of losing it."

"Fortunately, we also made a few friends there. We came to know people in our same horrible predicament, people who had also lost everything and had been separated from their loved ones. We did not know whether we would ever see you again, either," he sighed, and smiled at the women. He was so grateful that they had taken him in.

"Hetty and I were both so glad that we managed to meet some furriers and their wives whom we knew from The Hague. Do you remember the Smits? Three brothers who ran a fur shop downtown? We were only colleagues before, but now we befriended each other. Lena Smit and her daughter, Lisabelle, were together with Hetty in the women's camp. Most people we met had been immediately separated from all of those they had arrived with. Some had large families and had been deported to different camps; many had no idea where their husbands or wives were. They had lost track of one another. All of them had been taken from home by force, like we were. I was devastated when I had to leave Hetty behind in Vught, but I cannot even imagine how lost and alone she must have felt."

Fritz paused now to silence the turmoil in his mind. No news from Hetty in one year had his soul aching. *Please tell me that she is all right*, he pleaded silently as he looked up toward the heavens. He was literally starved. Starved for food and starved for news of Hetty.

If Fritz had not had a picture of Hetty in his mind, always with him, close to his heart, he would not have survived the hell he had been through. Tears were now running freely down his cheeks. The women were silent, having no idea how to console a person who had survived what they could not even imagine. They listened and shuddered. Now they knew more of what could have happened to all the people who had simply vanished.

"When I arrived at Auschwitz I was really devastated," Fritz went on. "It's as big as a city. A great deal of thought had gone into building it. It seemed like an industrial camp, built in segments, with factories belonging to large corporations. Some sort of deal must have been made with them in trade for getting to use us as free slave labor. Some of us were put to work doing extremely hard labor, like digging in thick mud. Everyone was treated shamefully. Many others died of starvation and contagious illnesses like typhoid fever. Others died from the ever-present body lice. Many people died from the brutality alone, but others just could not cope with the physical strain, the lack of sleep, and lack of food. There were many fatal accidents caused by the dangerous work conditions and, of course, exhaustion. Some even committed suicide by throwing themselves into the electrified fences."

He paused a moment, brooding. The women fidgeted. Finally, Fritz looked up and said quietly, "I just can't picture Hetty having managed there all by herself."

But he was already formulating a plan about how he would start his search for her. "Tomorrow, I will start writing to the Dutch consuls in other countries. Maybe she is stuck somewhere. I will go to the Red Cross and check the lists of those who have surfaced."

The women poured cups of tea and brought sugar. Fritz told them he had learned that most trains leaving Camp Vught went straight to Auschwitz. "Those who were alive when they arrived had become zombies when they left, if they ever did, and most did not." That is where the crematoriums worked around the clock, where Jews were gassed and burned in ovens. Everything there was built to extinguish us, and we, Jewish prisoners, were forced to build it all ourselves for that purpose. How could a place like this even exist?"

The three Van Dyke women sat listening in shock and awe. They had heard enough rumors, but until Fritz came to give them details, nothing had been confirmed. It was all too awful to believe.

"At least I am a free man again," he said.

Olivia, Sally, and Fleur were all horrified and captivated by his story, and after taking a break, they encouraged him to go on.

"In all of the camps there were enemies," he said, "even in Camp Vught. Some of the inmates were called Kapos." He described how Kapos were also the enemy. He explained how the Kapo system operated in the camps and how life threatening they became because they lived in the barracks with them and were as ruthless as the Nazis.

He said that, although most of the Kapos were convicted criminals, given reduced sentences for guarding and spying, some of them were even Jews themselves.

"They had been instructed to monitor us. We were always being followed and could feel eyes on our backs," said Fritz. "We were hungry all the time. The Kapos often had kitchen duty, which is how we learned to detect who was secretly patrolling us."

"We slept in three-level wooden bunk beds without mattresses at Vught," Fritz said, "with only straw on the bunks. The barracks had a strong smell, the combination of dirty clothes, dirty bodies, excrement, and stale moldy hay; but that was the least of our problems, and we got used to that smell quickly. We received one uniform per person. There was no detergent or anything to wash clothes with. Nothing. There were ten toilets, without doors, in the washrooms, there was never a moment of privacy. No warm water ever."

"We were allowed to have cold showers only once in three weeks," he went on. "When it rained, the washroom floor was flooded and icy cold. We were permitted to wash our clothes in the cold showers. We decided among ourselves to take turns drying the clothes for each other. We traded off who would rotate staying up all night by the one furnace in the corner and wave the laundry back and forth in front of it. Sometimes, we had to put our damp uniforms on in the morning. We hated it, but this was the way of life in the camps. Auschwitz, and its subcamps, well, I will tell you about that another time."

Could the Van Dykes even understand what it was like? Who could imagine having to subdue rage and accept brutal treatment, if only to live one more day?

Fritz looked into the ladies' sad eyes. Fleur and Sally were even more undone than their mother – and he felt somehow guilty for not having rescued others from the brutality of the camps and the viciousness of Hitler's regime.

Fritz said, "Kapos were willing to do dirty work for the Nazis for food, for an extra piece of bread. Imagine killing someone for a link of sausage? They guarded us and squealed on us, betrayed our confidence. Most of them were becoming hardcore criminals due to the way they chose to justify their inhumane deeds. They chose to be like their captors by helping support the Nazis' violence and inhumanity."

"Some inmates stole from one other," he explained. "Enemies were lurking everywhere. It was best to stay invisible and not speak out. There was no time for thinking because we were always on our guard. Always kept busy. Many of us slept terribly, as a result. Even after twelve-hour work shifts, we were exhausted during the long roll calls early morning and night. We were always mentally struggling to keep some thoughts at bay."

"When you lose hope, it doesn't take much more before you want to give up, and, after a while, you come to welcome death."

19

HETTY, JULY 1944

HANS LEAVES, HETTY SUMMONED

Flashback to 1942

Hetty's sleepless night was now triggering memories of her father. She berated herself for disobeying him so often and felt remorse for being a difficult teenager, always so defiant and unruly, even though her soft-spoken father had rarely lost his temper with her. She felt she could have been nicer to Hans, too. A few years back she begged him to introduce her to his new friends and always wanted to tag along with him, which he had graciously discouraged. Sometimes guilt at her shortcomings degraded the good memories.

Hans, at just 22, had been summoned in spring 1942 to relocate to a work camp – only about a month before Hetty had met Fritz. Young lads had been rounded up at random before. They still trusted the Nazis' promises, wanting to believe the lies about good working conditions and the promise of an attractive salary. Hetty came home one afternoon surprised to see her brother on the stairs all dressed up. Hans looked debonair in his navy-blue gabardine coat, a duffel bag hanging off one shoulder.

Hans was winded when they encountered one another in the stairwell. Hetty asked, "Where are you going, all dressed up like that?" He explained that he had received orders from the Jewish Council and was expected to appear at Central Station for travel right about now. He fished the summons from his pocket for her to read: "Be prepared and ready for travel to relocate for work. Bring warm clothing, valuables, money, and your I.D." Hans pointed his thumb to the satchel hung over his shoulder. As he ran off, he shouted back to her, "Tell father, too! I will send you my new address as soon as I arrive." She was so stunned that she said nothing; just stood there and watched him leave.

That was the last time that she or her father ever saw Hans. Hetty regretted that she had not given him a proper goodbye, and she could not get the image of Hans in his gabardine coat out of her mind. It was one of those images that belonged in her Memory Place, one that she treasured. She vowed to keep searching for Hans wherever she went.

On July 17, 1942, Hetty was to show up at the Nazi headquarters on Plantage Middenlaan in Amsterdam She had received the summons just a few days before. She had spent some hours packing on the 16th, ready to comply. The first group of adults summoned were single women, as well as single mothers and their children. They were to meet at the Hollandse Schouwburg, an old theater located in the middle of the Jewish quarter. It had been set up as an interrogation center, across the street from the children's day care center. All summoned Jews were to assemble there for the alleged purpose of "relocation and employment."

The women were required to show up, ready for travel, with some money and a few valuables, similar to what Hans had been told a few months before. This transport would send the women by train, wherever their labor was needed. They were told they would receive good pay and housing, and they assumed that they would be free to come and go as they pleased. This was one huge lie, of course, but one of the first official deportations that took place about two years after the war broke out. These young women were preparing to show up willingly because the climate of resistance had not yet taken hold and no rumors about extermination camps had yet reached their ears. But that was about to change.

The Resistance movement had begun in 1941, initially comprised of a few cells of the Communist Party, some church groups, and other independent groups. They became more organized as the war progressed, working hard to infiltrate Nazi gatherings and spy on them. The Resistance included many men and women who were willing to do anything to stop the Nazis. Fritz was one of several Jews invited to attend an urgent meeting at short notice because there was disturbing news to report.

At that time, no one had entertained the idea of not obeying Nazi orders because the Jewish Council was involved. The community of Jews trusted them. No one thought they may be complicit in the plan to exterminate Jews. However, when the majority of men and women of the Council were reluctant to meet the Nazis' demands, the Council director felt obliged to obey. The council regarded the process of informing the Jews of new restrictions placed on daily life as their duty, but refused to acknowledge the gravity of the plan to the community. If any actions or complaints were to reach the Nazi commanders, or if the Jews continued to resist, the board's family members would ultimately pay the price for disobedience.

Those threats worked. The Council continued to provide more than just the addresses and other information needed to facilitate the deportations, it used its own stationery to make it look like they supported the Nazi demands. Hetty's summons was typed on the Jewish Council's own stationery, hand-delivered by a Council member, and she, like many other women, was inclined to believe that the proposal offering "employment, lodging, and a salary" was legitimate.

Most Jews had lost their jobs under the pretense that there was plenty of work for them elsewhere. This deception was why Hetty had been dismissed from her job at Paramount Pictures in the first place.

The information given by the Nazis sounded reasonable, and Hetty had little choice in the matter anyway. Now that the summons had come, she had decided to go. She had little time to arrange for an alternative. She did not think she had any other option but to show up, because, otherwise, the police would come looking for her and would harass and maybe arrest her father.

Two types of propaganda films were being widely distributed. One was for the general public to turn their sentiments from tolerance to abhorrence of the Jews. Jews were not allowed to see those films. The other type of film was made especially for Jews to lure them willingly and unknowingly to slaughter.

The strategy of these films showed the detainees smiling – forcibly. These (imprisoned) people were seated at a workplace in their own clothing, sewing, working on an assembly line, or in the kitchens cooking. They were all nicely dressed, well fed, and looked cheerfully into the cameras. They were fooling everyone, making the work camps look attractive. They gave everyone the impression that nothing out of the ordinary was going on inside the camps. They had posed as willing participants when, in actuality, it was all a scam. This tactic worked for quite some time.

When people were summoned, they came of their own accord. Going to a Dutch work camp seemed to Hetty a nice place to learn clothing design, and if she didn't like it, she thought she could return home. She believed she could always communicate with Olivia and the girls and with whomever she wanted to in the outside world.

20

FRITZ, JUNE 1945

THE SECRET WEDDING

Flashback to 1942

That night, before retiring, Olivia gave Fritz clothing that had belonged to Sally and Fleur's father. When her husband had died, Olivia and the girls wanted to keep some of his nice suits that were in good condition. During the war, many items had been given away or sold when finances suffered, but the Van Dykes insisted that Fritz keep the clothing. He was grateful to them, as he possessed nothing and would otherwise be forced to continue wearing the striped prison uniform he had arrived in. He would no longer be stigmatized if he were wearing normal clothing. The shirts, trousers, and suits all turned out to be a good fit, and he was happy to regain a feeling of dignity when he saw himself in the mirror. It reminded him of how he had looked before the war.

It had been quite a while since he had worn normal clothes. He suspected that showing up in a suit with a look of self-respect would help him get his old job back at the De Klein company if at all possible. That is, assuming his former boss, Menno Librahm, the husband of his first cousin, Mathilde, had survived. He hoped that

Menno and Mathilde were back in their apartment on the Minervalaan, free again. He made a mental note to go and check on their whereabouts and see whether the factory was functioning again under their ownership.

He lay in bed that night remembering how he wanted to be dressed to the nines on his wedding day, but he'd had to be careful not to stand out while walking down the streets of Amsterdam. He lay there struggling with his emotions concerning Hetty. Yes, they had defied the enemy a few times, but could he have done more? Could they have gone into hiding themselves? Or saved anybody else? Was any of the suffering that followed his fault? Looking at his current situation, he concluded: *I am alive, but I'm alone.* He knew he needed to be realistic about the future. He lay reminiscing what had led up to his sudden and unexpected wedding day.

Fritz had been totally unprepared for the shocking news he heard at the clandestine Resistance meeting held on the evening of July 16, 1942, the night before Hetty was to report to the Hollandse Schouwburg.

Fritz met secretly with his Resistance comrades late that night in the unlit attic room of a residential building in a restricted area of town. He ignored the eight o'clock curfew that had been imposed on the Jews and had managed to avoid being caught. Through the shadowy canals of Amsterdam, he moved purposefully, watching his back for Nazi soldiers and spies.

The Resistance had started small, but it was growing. Some brave Dutch citizens were willing to risk everything to undermine and stop the Nazis. This included a network of people willing to hide Jews or blacklisted Resistance workers. A captured host caught hiding Jews or facilitating an escape was always dealt with severely. Anyone working in the Resistance was tortured to give up the names of other workers, and they too would be shot. For any single offense, 30 people might be publicly slain, execution style, to dissuade others from disobedience.

One of the tasks of the Resistance volunteers was to spread pamphlets throughout the Jewish community. Besides helping to find hiding places for persecuted individuals, Hetty's cousin, Rina Polak, was one of those who took great risks to inform the underground cells about what was going on in the news and of specific Resistance-related information. The pamphlets were printed on underground printing presses. Bulletins and newspapers about the state of the war were secretly distributed. Special compartments were sewn into corsets and worn under garments exactly for this purpose – along with concealing the transport of weapons.

Rina had decided to go into hiding in Rotterdam for a while. However, her need to fight against injustice inspired her to leave her hiding place and resume helping the Resistance. She spread pamphlets around the southern regions of the Netherlands, having decided that she had little to lose, and she risked her life on several occasions. Even though she was Jewish, she had blonde hair and a turned-up nose and got by the inspections with ease. She only had a bike with wooden tires, like many citizens. Rubber was scarce, and when the tires became worn, many people rode around on bikes with wooden tires that might soon break down and were heavy to pedal. No Jew had a bike by then, and the Nazis never questioned the legitimacy of her fake papers.

Only moonlight lit the worried faces at the meeting place that night. Fritz listened very carefully to the news as the new members looked at each other in shock. Apparently, horrific things were happening at the Nazi headquarters, and even worse in concentration camps in Eastern Europe. There had been rumors about the actual situation in the so-called labor camps, even in the Netherlands. The three Dutch labor camps were also transit camps. A stay in a Dutch transit camp was always temporary. Railways were being brought right into the center of the camps so that no one in nearby villages would witness what was going on. There were training camps set up to train Dutch civilians for guard duty where insane maltreatment of the Jews was the method of controlling them.

Fritz was told that most of the young unmarried Jews now being summoned to Nazi headquarters would be eliminated in extermination camps, perhaps on the day of their arrival. *What?* He wasn't sure he had heard right. The Resistance had spies in high places who had heard about the sinister extermination camps functioning in Eastern Europe, built for the sole purpose of murdering Jews. *What?* Is that what was really happening to all the people who were being rounded up? Is that what had happened to all those who had already disappeared? What had happened to Hans? This alarming news was not only hard to believe but required immediate action of some kind.

The Nazi propaganda had worked. They had been able to deceive the Jews into thinking that boarding a train and working for the Germans elsewhere would be just fine – it all looked innocent enough. It was devastating for Fritz when he learned he had fallen for their treachery and had been fooled by their lies.

Fritz knew that Hetty believed she had to comply with the order the next day. What choice did she have? Fritz's mind was spinning. Did the Jewish Council know what was happening in these camps? Rumors were circulating that the camps in the Dutch towns of Westerbork, Amersfoort, and Vught were actually prisons. In fact, there were two kinds of workers: forced laborers composed of non-Jewish young adults living under relatively normal conditions, but also slave laborers who were mistreated, starved, and worked to death – or sent to their deaths.

Fritz listened as more shocking news was told.

The final destination would be a death camp. Children were taken away from their parents, then gassed in chambers made to look like showers as they clawed at the walls in a vain attempt to escape. Parents were selected according to their abilities to work for the German war effort, but under the very worst of conditions. There was a drop-dead policy for workers because trains arriving daily could replace the "human freight" that died. His mind reeled as he heard about the gas chambers and mass graves.

Fritz was having a panic attack. He thought about a few family members who had already been summoned for this same transport. No one had liked the idea of going, but they were afraid to disobey orders.

Were all of these stories just rumors? For Fritz it all came down to believing this news and not losing Hetty. If these atrocities were indeed being committed, Fritz would have to do something to save Hetty. How could he convince her not to go to the Hollandse Schouwburg for questioning tomorrow? What could he say or do now that it was nearly too late to do anything? Still, these stories had to be taken seriously.

The truth of what he had to do started sinking in; the gravity of the situation was unmistakable. Deportation meant death! Then came a solution out of nowhere that calmed them all down for the moment and once again, Fritz's mind was flying in all directions.

The Resistance members came prepared with a solution for the warnings they had just conveyed. His friend, Stan Davids, convinced Fritz that he must marry Hetty immediately in order to save her life. *But how?* Fritz received detailed instructions on what to do next. Leaving the meeting, he once again remained in the shadows, creeping along dark streets and alleyways in search of the address he had just memorized.

It was long after midnight when Fritz found the front door he had been given by his Resistance comrades. Judge Visser was apparently willing to help Fritz and other people in a similar predicament. When he knocked on the door in the middle of the night, Judge Visser was wide awake and dressed in a three-piece suit as if he had been expecting Fritz. Visser told him that only legal documentation of their marriage could exempt Hetty from having to be put on transport the next day. Fritz gave Judge Visser all the required information to unlawfully predate the nuptials by at least 14 days.

He instructed Fritz to go tell Hetty immediately, then find a witness and appear together with Hetty in the ballroom of the Artis Zoo the next afternoon at 1:00 p.m., where he would marry the couple himself.

Just before Fritz left, Judge Visser told him, "Fear can be changed into something else. It can turn into courage. It can turn into purpose. It can turn into determination." He was clearly one of the Resistance members. He told Fritz to make haste and remember that the wedding must remain a secret. He must not breathe a word of this to anyone else.

By the time Fritz got home, dawn was breaking and he still had to sneak around in order not to be seen. Adrenaline was coursing through his veins, and he felt sick from the whole ordeal and the risks involved. What he had heard that night had deeply frightened him and had challenged his bravery. He left a note in Hetty's hallway urging her to come over so that he could tell her what had transpired at the meeting.

Hetty was so stunned that she did not know what to say. She had known Fritz for only nine weeks. Of course, she realized that time was of the essence, and because she was so very much in love with Fritz, she agreed. She then busied herself to find a witness. She decided to ask a dear friend, a non-Jewish former classmate, Astrid, to come to the Artis ballroom at the appointed time to witness the ceremony and sign the papers. But would she keep the secret? Hetty chose a simple two-piece suit to wear because it would be inconspicuous.

Hetty and Fritz tried to be casual as they approached the Artis Zoo, which just happened to be diagonally across the street from the Nazi headquarters. Soldiers were milling around outside, smoking, and laughing among themselves. Fritz and Hetty had discussed the risks and tried to appear relaxed, acting the part of a couple strolling down the Plantage Middenlaan with purpose but without destination; but they were tense knowing what was at stake. As they strolled, they were shaking inside. As they arrived at the entrance, more couples were coming from all directions. Altogether there were 120 people married that day, all sent there for the same reason by Judge Visser, for a flash wedding. This moment was monumental for both Hetty and Fritz and would change the course of the war for them, at least for now.

They were in a hurry, yet the ceremony was delayed. Hardly any witnesses had arrived. Hetty's nerves were causing her heart palpitations. She did not see Astrid anywhere. Everyone was whispering and tense. Had all the witnesses been too frightened of the possible repercussions? It was difficult to believe that the weddings were taking place with so many German soldiers patrolling nearby. If news of this had leaked out or if any soldier suspected wrongdoing, the consequences would have been horrific.

Luckily, one woman stood up. Edith Vos saw the urgency of the situation and offered to become everyone's witness. After saying their vows, Ms. Vos rapidly signed the predated marriage licenses so that proceedings would go on, and the group could disperse. Hetty was now no longer required to show up at the Nazi Headquarters that afternoon. If they came looking for her, she could prove that she did not belong to a group of single women. They all prayed that their secret would never be revealed.

It was miraculous that such a large group had gotten away with obtaining forged and predated documents without anyone being caught or hurt that day. It was a moment of hope, of defying the Nazis and establishing a slice of freedom amidst so much wickedness.

If Hetty had gone on the transport for which she had been summoned, she would have been killed. No one who departed that day would ever return or be heard from again. Nearly 2,000 women and several hundred children perished. Who could have foreseen that this could happen? Who could have known that each summons meant death? Or that the term "evacuation" was code for "elimination?"

After July 17, 1942, many deportations would take place, systematically, often, and regularly, sometimes twice a week. No relatives knew about or could have attended the ceremony without risk to them all. Luckily, when Fritz and Hetty returned home to tell Hetty's father, he was very happy for them. Yet they all still had an odd sense of unease, because there had been so many couples and so many witnesses, any of whom could still relay this information to the Nazis, even if only by accident. "Feelings of danger always undermine a sense of victory," Fritz thought.

Uncle Benno had not been home when they arrived at Fritz's apartment that afternoon. Fritz had spoken to his uncle early that morning and relayed the news of his meeting with the Resistance. He had intended to discuss the new living arrangements with Uncle Benno soon because, now that he was married, Fritz hoped for more privacy so he could be alone with Hetty, which otherwise would be difficult in a one-bedroom flat. What was odd was that Benno didn't come home that evening. Nor the next day.

They had been intent on letting him know of the nerve-wracking wedding and about the large crowd that had joined in, but after a week, Benno had still not returned. There had been no note, which had given Fritz pause. Had Benno been taken away by the Nazis?

There was nowhere to go to find answers for missing persons. There was never any closure possible.

Marriage had given Fritz and Hetty hope. They made a pact that day, a commitment "till death do us part." They had no idea how literal it was to be, and how soon that commitment would be challenged; yet this shared vow empowered them. Each evening Hetty waited until Fritz returned from work. He still had his job, though his salary had been reduced by 75 percent. Hetty gladly cooked for them, and they ate dinners together, uplifted by the delight that bled into their lovemaking each night.

On September 1, 1942, less that two months after Hetty and Fritz's secret wedding, Martin had come for dinner at their apartment down the street. They had enjoyed sharing one of Hetty's meals – it happened to be a Friday night routine with the three of them.

When Martin prepared to leave, he glanced at his wristwatch and noticed that it was past the curfew. He had planned to leave earlier, but they had all lost track of time. No Jews were allowed out after 8 p.m. The streets in the Jewish ghetto were constantly patrolled by Nazi soldiers driving around in jeeps and trucks, looking to intimidate or arrest anyone who did not adhere to the strictly imposed regulations. Although Hetty suggested that her father stay overnight on the couch, Martin insisted that he would be fine. It was just a few hundred yards' walk back to his own place. He put on his hat and his long coat with the yellow Star of David stitched to his breast pocket. He double checked to see that he had his ID papers handy and patted his chest as he smiled at Hetty. "No worries, thanks for a lovely evening. I will be careful." Then he turned to go, shutting the door behind him.

The next morning, Hetty walked down to her father's place to check on him and discovered that he had not come home. His bed had not been slept in. She became frantic and inquired at the neighbors' whether anyone knew where her father was. To her dismay, she was told that there had been a street raid in front of his door the night before, and that the Gestapo, the Nazis' infamous and ruthless political police force, had taken him away in a van. The neighbor assumed that Martin was at the Hollandse Schouwburg for questioning overnight.

But as Hetty and Fritz thought he might be detained for much longer, they prepared a package with food and some overnight necessities for him. With Fritz by her side, she walked over to the Nazi headquarters. When she arrived, however, she was denied entry. No one would take her package or give her any information about Martin Golden. She protested, insisting that she needed to speak to him, but to no avail. The door was slammed shut in her face. She sensed that something was terribly wrong, and she could not stop sobbing on the walk home.

Hetty was never able to shake that aching feeling of guilt for letting her father go home after curfew. She was haunted by the thought that it was her fault and that she could have prevented his arrest. "*If only I had insisted that my father stay over that night.*"

The image of her smiling father reassuring them and closing the door behind him was also set firmly in her Memory Place right next to that of her brother, Hans.

Martin and Hans had both been gone for some time, and now that Fritz was gone too, she was constantly filled with the loss of her loved ones. Sometimes unconsolably miserable. She was at a loss for solutions. She felt bad not knowing how to hate, nor whom to hate and hold accountable for her misery. During the day, she had found herself relying on The Memory Place more often, and each night she found some refuge there.

PART 3

OTHER WORLDLY

21

HETTY, AUGUST 1944

FIRST ARREST

Includes Flashback to January, 1943

The first time Hetty and Fritz were arrested was half a year after they were married, just a few months after Hetty's father had gone missing.

Life in the Netherlands drastically changed for Fritz and Hetty in 1943, even though they had always complied with the Nazis' wishes. They had bought many Jewish Stars of David to sew onto all layers of their clothing, from coats to undergarments, as was expected of them. Although this symbol stigmatized them, it also occasionally assisted Jews because, when recognized, it could help them find food and shelter. Fritz's connections in the Resistance were available for them if he needed assistance, and they believed that they were safe. They knew that life would undoubtedly get even more difficult for them in the future, but they had no way of escaping, so they were forced to adjust. All the borders were shut tight. If Rosalie and Richy had attempted to leave any later than they had, they would not have made it to Manhattan.

Hetty and Fritz had been summoned to come to the Hollandse Schouwburg in January 1943, and although they were really frightened, they complied. It seemed too late to find a hiding place now, at such short notice. Since the wedding, their neighborhood had been turned into the Jewish Ghetto of Amsterdam. Most Jews had already been evicted from homes in other parts of the city and had either been sent away or had fled here and were being held captive, contained in one neighborhood.

Being outside of one's home could be dangerous day or night, because along with an increase in Nazi sympathizers came the increase in surveillance. However, remaining indoors was by no means safe, either, because house raids had steadily increased, both day and night.

Hetty and Fritz were ordered to appear for questioning and have their personal identity papers reviewed on January 14, 1943. Neither of them had been in the Nazi headquarters before. The room was full of well-dressed Jews obediently waiting, sitting, or standing quietly. The atmosphere was tense, and the place was overcrowded. The armed soldiers intimidated them, walking around with their heavy boots noisily striking the theater's marble floor.

Those civilian Jews who could not fit into the room were sitting on the stairwell steps or leaning on the wall, all waiting for an interview with the Nazis. No one knew what was expected of them – or what they could expect.

Being here was even more disturbing than they had imagined. They had never expected to have to endure such a long wait in the absence of water and food. It would be 24 hours before their name was called.

When the Nazis grilled any of the civilians, the shouting resonated throughout the entire building, words echoing all around them. Most of the people whose interviews were over were escorted out by soldiers, one on either side. Hetty and Fritz got chills from watching the anguished faces of these people; they stared in silence, waiting.

Children whined. Nurses with long coats and white caps came in to take the children away, their parents told that their children would be across the street at the day-care center. They were told that they would be returned to them when the authorities were finished reviewing their papers. Hetty was so glad that she was not pregnant nor yet a mother.

Hours passed, and people were tired and unable to stand any more. They had slid down the walls and were sitting cross-legged on the floor. Most wore clothing that had likely been neatly pressed when they arrived, but were now rumpled; they were thirsty, hungry, and fed up with waiting. Nothing was given to them and their questions were ignored. Even more people were being ushered in behind them. There was a growing number of people lining the staircase, too, all waiting to use the only toilet available. Hetty recognized some of the people from her neighborhood.

One woman struck up a conversation with her. "Did you get the warning letter shoved under your front door?" she asked.

Hetty said, "No, we were summoned; what is the warning letter?"

"Here, read this. It came through our mail slot. We went home and waited and, a few hours later, we were picked up by soldiers and put in a van."

Hetty read, "Attention! It is imperative that you gather all your things together now, and arrive at the Hollandse Schouwburg tomorrow, by eight o'clock in the morning. Something has happened downtown, and for your own protection we will relocate you by train. That is all the information we can give at this point."

Hetty sat questioning why she and Fritz had not been told of an emergency taking place downtown. They had been summoned on the Jewish Council stationery. Could this have something to do with their forged wedding papers from six months earlier? All visitors came here totally unprepared for the dreaded outcome of the review, and Hetty and Fritz were extremely nervous thinking about what might await them.

Finally, a Nazi officer called their names, and, upon entering his office and presenting their documents, the man took the papers and promptly left the room. He stayed away for what seemed like ages. What was taking him so long to review those documents? Was something wrong with them? Had someone discovered something about the secret wedding or forged marriage license? Had the authorities somehow discovered something else? Had they discovered that Hetty's entire family had made an escape attempt before? A number of possibilities crossed her mind as fear grew, and the knot in her stomach tightened.

After what seemed like forever, the officer came back smiling, took a seat at the desk and stamped a large letter "S" for *Sperr* or "spared" across the first page of both of their ID papers and handed them back. The uniformed clerk then stood and told them that this was a permanent stamp and that they were free to go home. Just like that. They could leave.

Forty-eight hours after they had entered the building, they were standing outside again, hearts pounding in their throats and their minds racing. Fritz held Hetty so tightly she could barely breathe. The tension began to dissipate, sliding from their shoulders as they walked hand in hand down the street toward their apartment. Exhausted and starving, they quietly rejoiced in the knowledge that the Sperr was permanent. They needed to go home and to bed, but they wanted to go celebrate. They walked along the Amstel River stopping occasionally to hug and kiss each other, their sense of relief almost overwhelming. They wanted to share the news with Olivia, Fleur, and Sally, and headed toward their home instead.

As they approached, they discussed what the authorities had said and what they had not said. No officer had told them much about anything, only that their papers were in order. No one explained why they had been released and had received the Sperr. Both Hetty and Fritz deduced that it might have been because Fritz was still needed at his job working for the Germans. Even when many of his colleagues had been sent home and replaced by their German counterparts, Fritz had kept his job. He was still making fur-lined jackets for the German air force. Maybe no German furrier was skilled enough to replace him? Fritz ran four clothing and fur departments, and managed dozens of factory workers. Now that he had a permanent stamp on his papers, he assumed that he was useful to the Nazis. But there was never any assurance.

Hetty hoped and wanted to believe that this stamp would protect them for the entire war. They were relieved, but in the back of their minds something didn't add up. Something was nagging at them. Even though the populace knew nothing of the deception going on behind the scenes at the time, Fritz had once been warned, and they did not believe that the officer was being straight with them.

At the Van Dykes' home, Fritz and Hetty relayed the good news, and everyone clapped their hands to rejoice in their victory. The three women were living with their own stress, and this was a big event for them as well. They were always on guard because their world could come crashing down at any time.

After discussing it, they all reached the same conclusion, which was to rely on the protection the Sperr had given them. "We have been spared. We have the stamp to prove it. We just have to believe that this is legitimate, and they do mean what they told us today." Hetty said, "Let's just relax. I haven't relaxed since before the war started when our first escape attempt failed."

So, neither Fritz nor Hetty arranged to go into hiding, even though they may have been able to. They never asked the Resistance to help them find a hiding place; they decided to rely on their papers. The system of finding hiding places was very secretive, and most hosting families had enough space for just one person. Taking in more than one only increased the risk of attracting attention – and the risk of betrayal, and they did not want to be separated.

Living with strangers and without the possibility to communicate did not feel right, and it reinforced their decision to not find a hiding place, but to stay together in Benno's apartment. They then adopted a wait-and-see attitude. This would turn out to be the most regrettable decision either of them had ever made.

22

FRITZ, JUNE 1945

FRITZ ESCAPES

Includes Flashback to 1944

Fritz needed to relay to the Van Dykes how, even in seemingly impossible circumstances, one should never give up hope. He said, "I was surprised to find that when things could not look bleaker, something that seems initially horrible can bring about something good."

"That day in March 1944, I had been shipped out of Camp Vught by train to Auschwitz. Upon arrival when we passed beneath a sinister *Arbeit Macht Frei* entry sign my world became a nightmare. I never believed for a moment that 'work will set me free', which was what that German greeting on the sign meant. There, I was put to work for the IB Farben Company at Buna to make synthetic rubber. This company also manufactured the dreaded Zyklon B gas that was used for exterminating prisoners in those fake showers, but luckily, I didn't work for that department of the company."

The IB Farben plant was built in a subcamp of Auschwitz, one of 40 industrial plants that had been established in the region by the Nazis to offer German corporations cheap forced labor.

"Many of us were needed to build facilities there," Fritz said. "It was hard, grueling work. Many people, including friends, dropped dead from exhaustion. Others died or were crippled by accidents. Most of us were very weak, and our life expectancy was very short. They considered us expendable."

"After months of hard labor at Auschwitz-Buna under starving conditions and enduring harsh treatment, many of us became emaciated and were declared unfit; so, we were put on transport to Camp Buchenwald. Had you heard of this place? Most of us were sure it would be the end of us. We had heard rumors of extreme sadism happening there."

"There was a terrible blizzard on the day we left, and a large group of us were packed together, traveling in an open cattle car. Everyone was anxious. Those of us still able to think straight feared we were headed for an extermination camp. It was freezing cold, with gusty winds, and snowing hard. I had no shoes, and we were traveling at high speed."

"We were jammed together so tightly that nobody could move. There was nothing normal about this day, even for camp inmates. My teeth were chattering, I was trembling, my body was stiff. We all were freezing, and the only heat was the little amount of body warmth coming from the other men. I was despondent. I knew I would not survive this transport if we did not arrive somewhere and get shelter soon. Others were screaming and complaining about the icy cold."

As he spoke, Fritz relived the episode as if in a dream. How could he ever expect anyone to understand how depraved it all was? How could he relay the horror of it? He was shivering again, remembering how it was to be so close to death. It was unimaginable and far too painful to relive, but he knew he had to tell his story to someone.

"Then, I was assaulted by another inmate close to me, who had somehow gotten hold of a piece of wire. He was making grunting noises and saying unintelligible things, like he had lost his mind. Then he shoved me and started to bind my toes together with the wire, as if he were trying to cut them off! He was surprisingly strong, and I was struggling against him when other men joined in the scuffle. People were going crazy from the cruelty, hunger, and dehumanization. At first, a few men held me down, but then they started clawing at one another. The man with the wire continued to bind my toes, and I was in excruciating pain. I had no leverage and was screaming like a wild person."

"We were so cold and hungry that hope was all but lost. My immediate reaction to the pain was to press upward with my arms and, in no time, without considering the consequences, I stopped fighting, climbed up and over the men, grabbed onto the edge of the cattle car and jumped, floating for a moment among the snowflakes."

Luckily, the thick layer of snow in the wintry landscape by the side of the tracks cushioned Fritz's fall, and he rolled down a steep embankment until he stopped moving. Under normal circumstances, he would have been committing suicide by doing that. But because of the heavy snow, he'd survived. He limped and stumbled down the rest of the hill to a road. His feet were bare, and he had no belongings nor proper clothing, but he just kept moving, stunned to be alive. His jump from the train was more of a reckless act of madness than a rational act of bravery, but the result was the same. He had escaped.

"I was in a mountainous, uninhabited area and I walked for half a day," he said, "before I found a livestock shed on a farm. My limbs were frozen and numb, and I could not walk the next morning. I covered myself with hay and hid next to a cow, enjoying its warmth. When the farmer discovered me, he fed me well, and he bandaged my feet. I wish I could have stayed there, but I knew that as soon as he recognized that striped uniform, he'd be obliged to report me to the police. They were the ones who told me where the trains on these railways were headed.

The police officer who came the next day for Fritz treated him with more compassion than he had known in any of the camps. They took him to Landskrone prison, where he spent three weeks. "After that," Fritz said, "I was taken to Oskar Schindler's factory, which was in the Brünnlitz labor camp. It was so much better there than at Auschwitz. That is why I survived this stinking war."

"Arriving at Schindler's factory seemed like a godsend. At least Schindler became tolerant towards the Jews and later lenient with them. He secretly allowed Jews to celebrate the Sabbath in the barracks. That should give you an idea of how much more tolerant he was compared to other Nazis. We were liberated from there and I walked most of the way back here to you."

Fritz changed the subject now, wanting to share some good things as well. He thought, as bad as it gets, there are always good people and things that make you believe in something again.

"Some had their God to cling to in the camps," he told them. "Most believed in some God or a religion. Some were atheists, and some were not sure what to believe. It was a day-to-day process, and many people's faiths were severely challenged in the camps. Some thought that God had abandoned them. Their question was always the same: 'How can there be a God who allows this unspeakable cruelty?' Others said God was 'feeding' them, supporting them by giving them hope."

"Many, like me, had their own personal faith," he explained. "I made agreements with myself all the time to do what I needed to in order to stay alive. Sometimes it was impossible to keep my promises, but, once I found something to believe in and felt things improve, even a little, my outlook lifted."

"I chose a purpose to cling to. In my negotiations with myself – or with God – I cut a deal. 'Forgive yourself for the dreadful things you have had to do to survive. You need to forgive yourself for finding yourself in such a twisted, mind-boggling predicament that no one deserves to go through. You are not to blame.'"

Fritz broke down and wept for a few moments. Fleur and Sally gently stroked his back, and Olivia brought him a glass of water. When he had recovered somewhat, Fritz told them about the little things that had helped people stay alive in the prison camps.

"Many inmates helped one another," he recalled. "This behavior just comes naturally to good people, and it is just as contagious as evil behavior can be. Sometimes it made the difference between life and death. Like the guard who had been put to work outside the kitchen who had access to food. Her focus was on others. She would smuggle things out of the kitchen to help people suffering in the barracks. Once, other inmates distracted an officer from beating me for something I had not done. The inmates often watched out for those who needed help."

Fritz realized that if the man with the wire had not attacked him on the train in the blizzard, and if he'd not bailed out of that stock car into the snow and ended up at Brünnlitz, he would not be here today.

That train he had escaped from had been on its way to Buchenwald – the "Beech Forest" camp, which had been established near Weimar in 1937. Prisoners were sent there from all over Europe and the Soviet Union – Jews, Poles and other Slavs, the mentally ill and physically disabled, political prisoners, Romani people, Freemasons, homosexuals, and prisoners of war, as well as ordinary criminals. All prisoners were made to perform forced labor in local armaments factories, manufacturing and supplying ammunition for the war. The insufficient food and poor conditions, not to mention the daily executions, led to over 56,500 deaths at Buchenwald, of the estimated 280,000 prisoners who passed through that camp and its 139 subcamps.

Although the Buchenwald camp was not intended as an extermination camp, many thousands of people still died there. Its notoriety had reached his ears in the camps where Fritz had spent time, because the place was run by commander Karl Otto Koch, who was a mid-ranking commander in the SS and the first commandant of the camps at both Buchenwald and Sachsenhausen. From September 1941 until August 1942, he reigned as first commandant of the Majdanek camp in occupied Poland, stealing vast amounts of valuables and money from murdered Jews. His wife, Ilse Koch, participated in the crimes at Buchenwald and became known as "the witch of Buchenwald." She was known to have people killed on a whim. She also had a fascination with tattoos and would have those prisoners with tattoos skinned, using their dried and stretched skin to make lamp shades and other objects.

Fritz had every reason to be grateful that he'd never set foot in that camp – and for the chain of events that had led him to the farmer's wooden cowshed in the snowy mountains where he was fed and cared for. He was rejoicing now, knowing that it all lay behind him and that he was free. He had rediscovered a purpose and a way to survive. The jump from the train may not have been a successful escape at the time, but it had, in fact, saved his life.

23

HETTY, AUGUST 1944

SECOND ARREST

Hetty remembered the second time she and Fritz were arrested. It would turn out quite differently for them than the first one had. It had come as a complete surprise, on June 8, 1943, approximately six months after their first arrest. It had been nearly a year since Hetty and Fritz had wed, Hetty having thus far avoided a pregnancy and deportation. But betrayals had increased. More foreigners, ethnic groups, and Jews were taken on transports leaving for the camps on a regular basis. By this time, terror on the streets of Amsterdam was commonplace. The Nazis openly degraded, humiliated, and brutalized minority groups and Jews, using public displays to persecute them.

Most decent people were willing to comply with the Nazis and too afraid not to. Then there were the many collaborators, those who were willing to betray people for money. Some Jews turned in other Jews to save their own skin, but they were picked up and deported, nevertheless. By now, the true Nazi plans had surfaced and most people who had been reluctant to support the Nazis were pressured to become a member of the party in exchange for extra food stamps and privileges.

After radios were confiscated, any connection with the outside world was illegal and punishable. Hetty much later realized that she, too, might have been better off helping the Resistance than relying on the Sperr to keep them safe. Many residents managed to have secret radios hidden in attics and listened to the BBC broadcasts late at night.

Only a few dared not wear the Star of David or disobey the rules. Within that year, even though most Dutch newspapers were now in the hands of the enemy and reporting was not at all impartial, only a few people wanted to acknowledge the truth: that those who had gone off for relocation and employment were probably already dead and were never coming back.

One night, Hetty and Fritz were roused from a deep sleep by the sound of heavy fists pounding on their front door, accompanied by loud shouting. A few moments later they heard their door being broken down. Before they could even get out of bed, several uniformed officers from the SD (Sicherheitsdienst, a special branch of the SS) were standing in their bedroom. While shouting orders, the SD dragged them from bed by their arms. He told them to gather a change of clothes, then grab a coat and their pre-packed suitcases, which all Jews had earlier been ordered to prepare. Although the Dutch police were also there, they were assisting the Nazis with the forced eviction. The pounding on the doors was bone-shaking. Were other Jewish neighbors also being taken away? Had that stamp on their papers not been a legitimate "free pass," after all? Horrific screams could be heard blocks away. Then, several of the apartments were sealed, including that of Hetty and Fritz.

They were made to walk to the Nazi headquarters downtown in the middle of the night. Again, they waited for hours until their case was reviewed. Hetty and Fritz clung to each other, mortified over what was to come. They now knew that they should have tried to find a hiding place. It was too late, and the thought was killing them. Nothing in the Nazis' plans was random. The promise of a permanent Sperr had been effective enough to distract them from planning an escape of any kind; it had deterred them from going into hiding, while all along the Nazis knew that all promises were meant to be broken and were.

After three terrifying, hungry days and nights of waiting in the Hollandse Schouwburg, Hetty and Fritz were crammed into a crowded train compartment and taken on a three-hour journey straight to Camp Vught. The Nazis' treachery and lies was for many the greatest shock of all. Somehow, Hetty and Fritz had pushed away suspicions of a diabolic scheme, but they had known at some deep level that all the promises, even the signed and stamped kind, were lies. When a Nazi was agreeable to something, it was always temporary and was used to quell disturbances. Eventually, the Nazis' guise of being reasonable vanished and they became outwardly brutal, imposing more cruelty than necessary. Fritz and Hetty now believed all the rumors they had heard. But what could they do now? What was meant by a "transit camp, anyway?"

They would soon find out.

24

FRITZ, JUNE 1945

THE MEMORY PLACE

Fritz and the women spoke throughout the night, and though fatigue was catching up with them, nothing in the world seemed more important than this conversation. It was a joyous reunion studded with painful memories – along with some soothing ones. Fritz had come to the point that he wanted to share with them the greatest miracle of all.

"Just to stay sane, I can create a little space in my mind – The Memory Place, Hetty and I call it; it is a place to hide. Everyone can do it. Hetty did it too. It is a place to go where you block out your surroundings and try to take control of your conscious mind. You feed your unconscious mind instructions to tune out the worries, the hardships, the losses, and all the pain. I used this often during the long roll calls that could go on for hours. Or I would go to my Memory Place after the lights in the barracks went out at night and it was quiet. Lying in my bunk, I would go to my silent Memory Place, a magical place for my mind to rest."

"It is a sacred place in your own mind and heart. Even when your dearest people are beyond the veil, you can bring them back to life in

The Memory Place. And this works both ways – by remembering to keep them alive, your loved ones strengthen you, keeping you alive in return, wherever they are. It is a temple where your loved ones linger. The Memory Place is like prayer, only more real," he said.

Fritz told them, "Loving people from the past, in the present, and in the future is not enough. Believing – that is what you need. A reminder of why life is worth living, always."

"When I talk with her," he continued, "it relieves my heart. I feel her as if she is alive. Even though I cannot touch her, my heart swells and I can feel her presence. She is well dressed, looking like the stylish beauty she is, sitting in the bay window where I saw her for the first time, and that is the only place I feel safe, sometimes. No one can see me or monitor me there. Somewhere along the way I doze off. The next morning, I am often refreshed, until the back-breaking labor needs my attention. Or if a nightmare has awoken me. I revisit The Memory Place as often as I can."

Fritz explained, "We kept saying to one another: Just believe you can go there; imagine we are sitting at a large, round table enjoying a meal together, where hope and faith are generated and still live."

"Hetty and I made a vow: If we get split up, save my image there. Try to remember my face and smile when you see it. See only beautiful things and know that this pain will be over soon. There is one certainty in life, which is that everyone dies, and everything will come to pass. One way or another, the war will end. Have faith that I will come back to you."

Fritz took a moment, then he looked up at the women with watery, questioning eyes and whispered, "Where are they all now?"

The air was thick with silence. No one was able to speak.

"I, for one, have felt the power of hope that comes from her love for me. The thought that Hetty kept her faith in me brought me back here to you now."

All four of them sat mourning their own losses while thinking of Hetty. "That is all I have to build upon." Fritz told them. When he looked up this time, a spark of determination was stirring, and he spoke resolutely. "I will start looking for her tomorrow. I won't stop until I find her."

PART 4

WORLDS COLLIDING

25

HETTY: JUNE 1944

CONTRACTING DIPHTHERIA

The days in Auschwitz had seemed like a lifetime. Hetty, now exhausted and in agony on so many levels, still felt a sense of relief when she and the people she worked with from the Philips group had been put on transport to a new destination. That destination was Camp Reichenbach. Some people had gone on transport to different camps, but Hetty was once again fortunate for being on a train with the few people to whom she had become attached. One of these people, whom Hetty had met and worked with at Camp Vught, was Dottie Kaplan, a German Jewish lady who had been living in Amsterdam when the war broke out.

Dottie, a German-Orthodox Jew in her late twenties, had been raised in a town full of other observant orthodox Jews. Her family had never really mingled with non-Jews – not even with reformed Jews. She was religious in her upbringing and strict in her faith. Hetty had been raised differently, being from a liberal Jewish family who had integrated with many folks of another faith. Her upbringing was quite liberal. Dottie had been raised in an upper middle-class household, was older than Hetty, and was better educated. Dottie was also very disciplined. She was as committed to surviving as much as Hetty was.

Getting attached to someone was risky, however. You might just be willing to die for someone who needed your help – even if you hardly knew the person. Everyone who had your back also deserved your protection and support. This rule was an unspoken code among inmates inside the camps. On the other hand, nobody could be completely trusted, and you needed to always be on guard. It was never a good idea to become dependent on another inmate because you were always on your own when it came to your own survival. You'd best avoid planning something with another who may, just from pure exhaustion, end up malevolent toward you or, even worse, dead. Still, the less alone Hetty was, the more likely she would survive.

On June 11, Hetty, Dottie, Lena, and 250 women left over from the larger Philips group had boarded trains to go to Reichenbach, where the Telefunken Electronics company was situated. It was now made known that 150 of her group had stayed behind in Auschwitz and most likely would perish.

Before leaving Auschwitz, Lena and Lisabelle had gone to the Sauna together for the "selection," but only Lena had rejoined the group. Lisabelle, the youngest of the Philips workers, had been ordered to stay behind. Lena and Hetty developed heartache as never before. They all thought Lisabelle was going to die, and they were devastated.

They knew that she was unwell; she had a cough and was a bit feverish. But Lisabelle was still young. Wouldn't her age exempt her from staying behind? Getting sick in a concentration camp was no option for an inmate, because that meant failing the next selection. Illness nearly always meant death. Hetty had no idea whether there was even a hospital here.

They finally heard from inmates arriving in Reichenbach much later that Lisabelle had been sent to the infirmary for quite some time. Lena was in such a state of despair that Hetty needed to hold her up for roll call. Even when Lena had offered to stay behind at Auschwitz to be with her daughter, this had not been granted. She could feel Lena's anguish dragging them both down, and it was unnerving. Hetty and Dottie had a full-time task trying to console her.

They all now focused their hope on Anna, who had promised Lena she would keep watch over Lisabelle. When the women left, many people joined them in weeping for loved ones who were forced to stay behind.

After two more days of travel in the same uncomfortable conditions as they had traveled to Auschwitz, they arrived at Reichenbach. As Hetty got down from the train, she looked around her. Adjusting to the new camp would take some getting used to, but she hoped it would be better here than at Auschwitz. Their barracks overlooked the Eulengebirge mountain range in bright sunlight. On arrival, they were then given a knife, fork, spoon, and a cup for water or soup. Every bed had two cotton blankets, and there was some food to eat, which was welcome after their long, miserable journey.

However, two days after arriving there, Hetty contracted scarlet fever. Scarlet fever is a very contagious illness that is a complication of strep throat caused by a bacterium and needs treatment. It is usually accompanied by a rash over the entire body and a red tongue. If this illness goes unattended, another more serious illness, called rheumatic fever, can develop, which can travel to the heart, joints, and brain. Hetty and her friend, Dottie, were both more than worried, picturing Hetty having to return on the next train to Auschwitz now that she was ill and likely considered useless. She needed medical care, but she was terrified at the prospect of having to set foot again in Auschwitz.

Happily, Hetty's luck held, and she was not returned to Auschwitz. After receiving care in the Reichenbach infirmary, she was returned to work with the Philips group. This gave them all hope, and they clung to the belief that one day, they would be freed.

26

FRITZ, JUNE 1945

THE QUEST TO FIND HETTY BEGINS

Hetty had good looks on her side, with blondish-brown hair, a cute, upturned nose, bright blue eyes, and an enchanting smile. Fritz was hoping that her appearance would have worked to her advantage. Not looking too Jewish could get her better treatment in the camps. Her features were not nearly as dark as most of the tribes that inhabited the Mediterranean coast or the ancestors of the Jewish people called the Semites, who originated in Mesopotamia.

Semite is an old term for an ethnic, cultural, or racial group associated with people of the Middle East, including Arabs, Jews, Akkadians, and Phoenicians. The storm of anti-Semitic violence loosed by Nazi Germany from 1933 to 1945 not only reached a terrifying intensity in Germany itself but also inspired anti-Jewish movements elsewhere. Anti-Semitism was promulgated in France by the Cagoulards, in Hungary by the Arrow Cross, in England by the British Union of Fascists, and in the U.S. by the German American Bund and the Silver Shirts.

In Nazi Germany, antisemitism reached a racial dimension never before experienced. Christianity had sought the conversion of the

Jews, and political leaders from Spain to England had sought their expulsion, but never before had a government suggested the murder of all Jews.

Hetty spoke and understood German fluently and could speak a little Yiddish – which is similar to German in grammar and with many similar root words. Not only had this proven helpful in her work at Vught, but she was also sometimes needed to interpret for other prisoners. Fritz hoped that her intelligence and talents, together with her language skills, would have impressed the Nazi authorities enough to spare her. "Was that just wishful thinking?" he wondered. Fritz had met many skilled doctors in the camps who were just eliminated at random. Did any Jew ever get a chance to impress a Nazi?

He hoped she had found some way to hold on to hope and stay well. With her bubbly personality, she made friends easily. She had kept the women in Vught amused by telling entire stories of the books she had read, in her lively manner. In her work at Paramount Pictures, she had seen dozens of feature films that most of the other women hadn't seen, and she would share her favorites with them, mostly romantic comedies. Fritz smiled recalling the joy in her eyes as she relived hilarious scenes in the movies; he loved her expressive laughter, and it echoed in his ears now.

She would have had miraculous moments of her own, too, wouldn't she? Of course she would, just as he had. Hopefully her Memory Place was filled with calming thoughts to smooth out the rough days. Like how prayer brings hope and answers in times of extreme need. Maybe she was on her way back to Amsterdam. Perhaps they would hear from her soon. Fritz was not planning to be passive, however; he was ready to go to great lengths to find her.

On his travels homeward, Fritz had run into Otto Frank, Anne and Margot Frank's father, who knew some of the same people Fritz knew. He remembered Otto from roll call. At Auschwitz, "Otto

Frank" and "Fritz Frankel" would often end up side by side, standing for hours, often whispering during roll call. Otto told him that the Germans had evacuated the last of the women's camp at Vught at the beginning of June 1944. That was about two months after Fritz had left there, which coincided with the date on Hetty's note that Olivia had saved for him. Hetty in Auschwitz? He was sickened inside.

Fritz was still bitter thinking about how people were forced to create and maintain the perverted values and rules that worsened the workload, increased the hunger, and turned everyone into beggars, thieves, and fools. Auschwitz was a place designed to eliminate millions, leaving no trace and no proper goodbye or burial. Only wretchedness and power-hungry criminals determining the fate of the weak and innocent. This way of thinking was devastating for Fritz, and it made him miserable, always knowing the nearness of death in Auschwitz-Birkenau and how the sights and smells would haunt him forever. Always knowing that there were many other death camps, like Chelmno, Belzec, Sobibor, Treblinka, Majdanek, and Mauthausen, just to name a few.

On the other hand, knowing Hetty's exact departure date from Camp Vught was good news, too. Now that he knew that date, he was more likely to pick up her trail. He told himself to remain optimistic. Perhaps she had been spared and had gone to a new camp where she was put to work, as Fleur had suggested, and as he had done. He made a mental note to see whether he could find someone who knew of the fate of that specific trainload of women. Maybe some of the women from Vught had survived and were already back in town? Maybe the Red Cross will know? Maybe some were in foreign places stuck without transportation back. Perhaps some were walking home? That could account for a delay.

Fritz went everywhere looking for Hetty and asked people he knew from the past whether they had news of those who had gone missing during the war. Olivia had suggested he read the Red Cross listings, because they were the most accurate and were centrally located in town.

Fritz was confident that some newly arrived war victims would also register at hospitals and clinics, and he became more optimistic knowing that there were more places to look. Who knows, perhaps he would find her name on a list of the wounded. He would go to all of the hospitals and clinics, if need be. He decided he would also write letters to every Jewish organization in England and other countries, places where lists of camp survivors were posted.

After dinner with Fleur, Sally, and Olivia, Fritz went up to his room in the attic, glad to be alone and at peace. He had gotten some more things off his chest, and it felt good to release his sorrow, or at least share it with these dear friends. But he could not help but think of Hetty, Hans, and Martin – as well as his own family, all of whom had vanished.

Fritz's insomnia gave him too much time to think. That's when the demons took over. But Fritz had taught himself while in the camps to enter a meditative state by returning to The Memory Place. He could picture Hetty laughing and holding his hand; he could feel the joy as if it had already come true. Time and again he realized he could rely on this and believe it, and he hoped that Hetty hadn't forgotten to believe it either. He prayed she had not given up.

Last night, he had pictured Hetty with him at a café in Amsterdam, enjoying each other's company, laughing together. Tonight, he pictured her as he had first seen her, sitting in the bay window, reading. Fritz imagined himself coming home from work, finding Hetty reading a book, ready to share a meal with him, and he drifted off to sleep.

27

HETTY, JUNE-DECEMBER 1944

CAMP REICHENBACH

Reichenbach was a camp run by the electronics company, Telefunken, and, like Philips, it made radio equipment. This company was provided with forced laborers who were paid nothing. Like in Camp Vught, many large German firms could afford to expand their production by building factories inside the camps. These corporations were all inclined to treat prisoners brutally; the work was both dangerous and exhausting, and no extra provisions were given to the forced workers for the dangerous risks they took on a daily basis. This was the third camp the women had found themselves in, and the size of their group would dwindle as time went on.

The Philips group of women realized that their former employer, Philips & Co., had most likely negotiated some exchange so that these women would be put to work here instead of staying at Auschwitz. This could be why they were permitted to leave after only a few days there, and why they had been told that they were "special freight." They were incredibly grateful to Frederik Philips. Maybe the man was no hero, but he had stepped up to the plate when it came to negotiating with the Nazis and cut a deal to protect them. They knew his efforts accounted for the special treatment. But it's also true that they had experience working with light bulb fixtures, and the products were similar to those of Philips.

Telefunken's complex at Reichenbach had been built underground to protect it from assault by air. Although Hetty had been hopeful at first that this camp would be far different from Auschwitz, it was not a whole lot better. The emaciated prisoners had to work nights; they had to walk to the factory in the dark and work underground from 6 p.m. to 6 a.m. The roll call and lack of food were the same here as at the other camps. Prisoners were all systematically underfed, overworked, and on the brink of madness. These forced laborers were meant to be worked to the bone – or beyond. Then, an outbreak of typhoid fever grew rampant and began claiming lives. Luckily, Hetty and her small group of friends survived it.

Hetty and Dottie tried to find blank pieces of paper, sometimes fetching scraps from the garbage, hoping to keep a journal. The women had a difficult time finding a pencil or pen, which none of them had, but they eventually managed to find the stub of a pencil which was enough to write with. They had no real possessions whatsoever, in fact – no toothbrush, safety pin, comb, or any other item except for an enamel cup. Finding time to write, when no guards or Kapos were looking, was hard enough. Smuggling a journal out of a camp was another matter altogether. They had no idea how they would manage it, but they felt the need to journal some of the most extreme and disturbing things they saw, because they thought, "How can we explain this to anyone?" Hetty had a very good memory and was able to remember the names and faces of the commanders running the camps. She also could sketch what the barracks and landscape had looked like. She did her best to remember what she might say if any of the officers were ever put on trial for their crimes. Hetty had thought that, at the trial, she would tell the facts and not get overly emotional because in her new reality, facts and truth had more power to convince than emotional outbursts do. These useful behavioral tips would come in handy then as well as in her acting career, she concluded.

If the journal was seized now, while she was still captive, there would be hell to pay. Yet, Dottie and Hetty were determined to somehow get their story out to the world.

Dottie noted the details of the camp in the makeshift journal: Although the work was performed sitting down, night work was very strenuous for everybody. Most of the women were already in a weakened condition, undernourished and on 12-hour work shifts, walking back and forth for an hour each way, often in the rain. There was always a lengthy roll call. All of this slowed the production of their work.

Soldiers marched behind them everywhere they went, always with guns and dogs. "Terrorists were always accompanying us wherever we went," wrote Dottie. "When I wanted to go to the bathroom, somebody went with me. What was considered a meal was issued at 11 p.m. A meal that needed to be consumed within 15 minutes. Once again, like before, the soup consisted only of water and potato peels. We would go back to work right after that. Germans, Russians, and Polish people worked with us there."

Newcomers arrived weekly in Reichenbach, some from camps other than Auschwitz, and some totally unprepared for the life they would lead there. Some came straight from home in plain clothes, who had been selected to work based on their skills, health and age. Some were only teenagers, girls who had been separated from their families. Hetty and the other women in the barracks sometimes told the newcomers of their own experiences and of how numb some of them had become. They also prepared them for how it was when the numbness made it impossible for them to think clearly.

Hetty and Dottie saw many women become completely dissociated. Some acted strangely, despite being able to do their work; they just went through the motions, obeying the bosses, but without being totally present. Lena was still anguished and depressed about Lisabelle. That is partly why Hetty decided it was better to tell newcomers what to expect, so they could conserve energy and find ways to stay hopeful and survive.

Hetty or Dottie would tell the young newcomers what they thought they needed to know about the suffering: "We have to work with arrogant prisoners who belittle us. The German factory workers here act as if they are greatly superior to us. They certainly get better food than we do. They think they are the big shots. The worst part is when, at noon, they unpack their lunch boxes full of delicious-smelling meats, cheese, and rolls. When you are so hungry that you are on the brink of madness, the delicious aromas of that food can nearly take you over the edge. Early each morning on our way back from our night shifts, we walk through a little village. We can smell fresh bread that probably just came out of the ovens. When you smell that, you almost faint from hunger. It is the worst kind of torture day after day. All we do is talk about food all the time. People in the villages often stand by the side of the road as we pass by, gawking at us. They know who we are. They see us all in our striped dresses, some of us shaven bald, and others with very short hair, forced to walk alongside the SS who are always marching with their dogs. You can just tell that they know that this is very, very wrong, for sure. Yet, they will not intervene; in fact, they shout nasty things at us. So far, wherever we have gone, neighboring villagers have acted unfriendly."

Hetty explained: "One thing is paramount in our minds. Do not get sick, because if you do, the truck will come for you. That truck is a mobile gas chamber – and you will be killed right there, on the spot. We have seen people go in there, and they don't come out. That is why we work hard and push ourselves to the utmost. Those who get sick or are in such a weakened mental state that they just don't care anymore end up being executed there, inside that truck."

"We are all young adults here at Reichenbach," Dottie told them. "The oldest are about 40 or 45. Some arrived with teenage children.

The kids have to be at least twelve years old to join their mothers here in the workforce. The younger children were left behind in Auschwitz to be eliminated."

Dottie added: "Most of us have begun acting like robots. We function automatically but are unaware of what we are really doing. I have the feeling that I am physically here, but everything else is gone. I cannot think clearly. I try to keep my sanity. You ask yourself, 'What was the name of my father again?' 'My mother?' 'What was my birthday?' Things like this are difficult to remember. Your mind does not function properly anymore. When I think about it, we are like bears in hibernation. We continue to live, but we do not eat anything, we are not entirely awake. The will to live seems like a separate thing. You don't know where the energy to survive comes from. You must be an extraordinarily strong person to find the will to live here. You get to the point that you don't talk to other workers – just to preserve your strength. Every word you say is a strain, a drain of your energy. I don't even want to eat the piece of bread I have, because it is simply too much work to open my mouth. Once my mouth is open, it doesn't close by itself."

"I must have gotten scarlet fever back in Auschwitz," Hetty told them, "because I did not notice I was ill until we had been in Reichenbach for a few days. Then I was put in quarantine in Langenbielau. I was so afraid I would be sent back to Auschwitz. I was separated from everyone and frightened. Things were really miserable in Langenbielau. There was barely any food, and all 30 of us with scarlet fever had to wash in the same bowl of water. This is an extremely contagious disease and comes with a burning sore throat and bad red body rash. We were treated very badly."

Around the end of December 1944, they had begun to hear a constant rumble approaching from the East – the Russian troops fighting and coming closer. The Nazi guards heard it too, and it made them nervous. Then came a Russian air raid, which bombed their camp. They had run for cover and, luckily, none of them were injured or killed. The approach of the Russians was just as frightening as the Nazi threat was to them. The bombing ultimately prompted the officials to start planning to move everyone to yet another camp, farther west.

Then, unexpectedly, a true miracle happened that was thoroughly unexplainable. This unexpected event outshined all the other happy surprises in the life of Hetty's campmates; it resonated many times through the hearts of all the women and men stuck there, and would forever send shivers down Hetty's arms whenever she spoke of it. It had a momentous impact on all of them, but most of all on Lena.

Anna had kept her promise – because it was six months since Lena had been in Auschwitz, and just like that, Lisabelle arrived.

28

FRITZ, JUNE 1945

RETRIEVING HIDDEN VALUABLES

Every afternoon, Fritz went to the Red Cross to check the listings. Hetty's name had thus far not appeared on any lists of the dead or severely injured. He had not found her on the lists of survivors, either; but he was convinced that, any day now, he would. One afternoon, Fritz ran into his distant cousin, Henry, who had been in hiding with his parents for nearly three-and-a-half years in Amsterdam South in a single, tiny, attic room. Henry and both of his parents had been sheltered by an elderly evangelical preacher who, out of the goodness of his heart, and without expecting anything in return, let the three of them live with him in his apartment upstairs. A group of Christians from the congregation had all joined in efforts to save Henry's family. The preacher hid them while others saved their belongings for them, and still others brought them food. They had risked their lives to do this. During the several times when the SS came to the apartment while they were in hiding there, they would run to hide in a crawlspace below the bathroom sink. Shortly after the war, the preacher had died, and Henry's parents had a tombstone made for him.

Henry told Fritz he had gone nearly mad living confined like that. Fritz realized that Henry had been living in a prison of his own. Henry and his parents had to be silent day and night – even footsteps were not allowed, because others also used the stairwell, and any movement detected by a stranger could be a death sentence for them all. They had been given a pail for a toilet and a pile of books to read. The preacher communicated with them by writing notes.

When the large Allied tanks clattered through the streets of Amsterdam and whistles of joy filled the air celebrating the liberation and the end of World War II, Fritz was still far away. But Henry spoke of how he and his parents had partaken of the beer that was flowing and the partying that ensued. He had run down the stairwell, screaming with joy, ecstatic, skipping steps in a rush to join the cheering throngs in the street. He told Fritz of the kilometers of tanks, flags, and happy people lining the road. Henry had promised himself that if he ever got out of that apartment, he would never ever go back upstairs. Never again!

Henry later was sorry he had forgotten his mug – the only souvenir he had wanted to keep. In his joy to be free, he had left it upstairs when he hastily left the apartment – but he'd kept the promise he'd made to himself and never went back. He swore to Fritz that his stay there had messed with his head. He felt as though he was held captive by invaders, by time, by war, and by the walls; but mostly by his parents, who always insisted he do things their way. He never wanted to speak of that place again. He experienced three-and-a-half years of that torture, which for a growing young man was damaging.

Fritz continued to walk to the Red Cross offices every day for more than a week and had read every survivor list they had, including a special list of prisoners who had died of typhoid, gangrene, or tuberculosis. Some had died after liberation day. *Imagine that, surviving all that suffering right up to Liberation Day, and still dying, never to return*, Fritz thought. He had been steadfast in his daily search for Hetty, yet he barely had the stamina to keep going. The

Van Dyke women noticed how fatigued Fritz was after long days of searching. No one else that he knew had returned. Some days he felt desolate and disappointed. "There must be more camp survivors," he assured himself. He just had to keep looking.

After Fritz had been home for days and had asked around everywhere for Hetty and other family members, he was at the Red Cross listening to a nurse reading names aloud and one name caught his attention. There was a Hetty mentioned – but with a different surname. Fleur had heard a broadcast on the Swedish radio with mention of a Dutch group called the Philips group, but Fritz had no knowledge that Hetty had ever worked for Philips, so none of them paid much attention to what was further being said about it then. There had been a contact address given, but it escaped their attention, and, anyway, Fleur was not sure whether the name matched. Fritz had no luck finding the address of a camp in Sweden, so he was not on alert to know more about who had been included in the Philips group.

"I won't give up looking," he wrote to Aunt Rosalie in America in a letter telling her he had survived. "In the next couple of days, I will go and retrieve the property we left behind at Benno's place. I am searching for Hetty every day."

As soon as Hetty and Fritz had understood what a street raid meant to those who were rounded up back in 1942, even before their arrests, they had started hiding important things. He had thought everything would remain untouched in their apartment and their belongings would be there waiting for them. How naïve they had been. He was planning to go back, but something prevented him from returning to their flat. He was nervous and scared.

Before they were arrested, Jews had been ordered to be ready to leave at a moment's notice, so they had packed overnight suitcases for that reason. But besides doing that they tried to save valuable bank papers, contracts, family heirlooms, and money elsewhere, so they hid many items behind some of the wall paneling in each room, then glued the panels shut. In the attic they hid items under the floor panels. Fritz had hoped nothing would be touched, but he was not an idiot. Everything they wanted to save was hidden well. Would it still be there?

They had also brought Martin's violins to a small musical instrument-maker's shop owned by a nice gentile man, Mr. Roland, who had made violins for him in the past. The old man was receptive to the safekeeping of the violins, bows, and cases.

Fritz had also brought a few of Hetty's nicest garments and some money for safekeeping to her girlfriend, Elly. Elly was the wife of one of Fritz's gentile friends, Niels, whom he and Hetty both knew and thought they could trust. A fur coat, one heirloom belonging to Bertie, and some family photographs were also brought to safety.

Fritz and Hetty thought they would only be temporarily detained somewhere, but they had imagined returning to reclaim everything and get on with their lives. They told only one person where everything was hidden, never assuming that their friends would take anything of theirs. But the Nazis had assured everyone that no Jews were coming back. It had been two years, and no one expected any Jews to return.

The Nazis gave the Dutch police stolen goods to guarantee cooperation, and many influenced their own friends to participate in the looting. The Nazis argued that Dutch citizens could profit and that looting was permitted. The Nazis encouraged destruction of Jewish property and were now offering the non-Jewish citizens better jobs available with better pay. Finer housing was available when the Jews left. The populace had been led to believe that since the Jews had gone, everything was up for grabs. There was a strict chain of command, and everyone on the chain would be rewarded with material goods. Many figured that refusal to accept these material gifts would be seen as defiance, so people justified owning things that were not rightfully theirs.

Fritz heard from Olivia's daughters that the new residents in Jewish homes would remove wall and floor panels in search of valuables left behind – which perhaps explains why returning Jews often received hostile reactions and were not welcome when they came back to retrieve their valuables. When Fritz went back to find things he had brought to others for safe keeping, he was angrily turned away. "That's just the way it is with money and things that people covet; it corrupts them," the Van Dykes explained.

Fritz did the rounds each morning like he did every day without finding Hetty's name – although he recognized the name Stan Davids, the Resistance worker he'd known who had helped Aunt Rosalie forge documents so that she and Richy could flee. Stan Davids had been at the meeting in the attic the night before the wedding. It was great news that he had survived, too. Even though he and other Resistance workers had been identified and blacklisted, they had gone underground. Fritz made a mental note to find him. Fritz would sometimes wait at the Red Cross just hoping for a familiar face, someone who might know someone who already returned who knew more about his relatives or something about Hetty, or about her departure from Vught, or some other news he could use.

One afternoon after his visit to the Red Cross, he went to the little music store. When he pulled the bell on the front door, Fritz heard the familiar voice of Mr. Roland. When he appeared the small gentile man immediately recognized Fritz, his face changing color, in shock at seeing Fritz alive. Then he started to cry. He gave Fritz a hug and asked, "How are you and the missus?" Fritz shrugged his shoulders, the look on his face revealing that he did not yet know. Mr. Roland asked Fritz whether he would come to dinner sometime, and before Fritz had even replied, Mr. Roland went into the back and brought him the violins that had been entrusted to his care. This decent man, a man Fritz barely knew, restored some of his faith in humanity, and Fritz never forgot him.

Later that day, Fritz met with Hetty's friend, Elly, the one married to Niels, with whom he had entrusted many of Hetty's dresses. Her face revealed how embarrassed she was to admit that she had worn some and given some others away because Hetty was never expected to return. Elly and Niels also revealed that they had spent the money Fritz had left with them. Fritz decided that he never wanted to speak to them again.

Fritz went to retrieve a fur coat he had made for Hetty, and the friends who had watched over the coat were happy to return it to him. Their kind expressions moved Fritz, but he noticed how no one asked about what he had gone through. No one knew an appropriate way to respond to war victims coming home.

Now that he had made some progress, Fritz planned to step right back into his old familiar life. Within a week, he had succeeded in getting his old job and some clothing back. His Jewish boss, Abrahm De Klein, had come out of hiding and had reclaimed his business. The man was relieved that Fritz had survived and was more than happy to have him return to work. Work, they both knew, was going to help Fritz stay sane.

He now had a chance at a new life. Starting all over again had its merits. The Fritz from before the war was gone forever, and he would never be the same man again; but the Fritz from after the war was a wiser and more knowledgeable man, and he had become a master at his trade.

29

HETTY, JANUARY 1945

THE GOOD SAMARITAN

After having survived six months at Auschwitz, Lisabelle had arrived at Camp Reichenbach in one piece. All the women in the barracks were overcome with joy for both mother and daughter. How incredible that they had been reunited. Lovely Lisabelle, with her head shaved, had one morning simply appeared at the camp barracks. She had been forced to grow up in a few months' time and learn to rely on herself – and it had of course, changed her. Lisabelle, the girl with the eyes of a survivor, came back to them a little older, stronger, and more mature. And yet, when Hetty looked into her beautiful face, she could see her pain. What had happened to her? Luckily, she was smiling. The women of the Philips group welcomed her with open arms, cries, and tears of joy. None of them could fathom how Lisabelle had managed to get out of Auschwitz alive.

She was shown into the barracks, and the women quizzed her about how she had survived. What kind of work had she done in Auschwitz? How was her stay in the infirmary? Did Daan's sister, Anna, help as she had promised? Hetty realized that she had witnessed the worst and the best days of Lena's life: the day that the mother had to leave a daughter behind in hell and the day that the daughter rejoined her mother again. Lisabelle was really back!

Lisabelle, so relieved to have found her mother and friends again, fell into her mother's arms; everyone could see that she had suffered greatly.

At Auschwitz, Lisabelle had met the "Angel of Death," himself, Dr. Josef Mengele. Survivors remembered his presence on the selection ramps at Auschwitz. He had gained notoriety as the killing doctor, a man who systematically performed evil experiments on his captives. He was known for conducting the most cruel and perverse surgical experiments on prisoners – without sedation of any kind. New prisoners were warned right away to watch out for him. He was particularly interested in performing sadistic procedures on twins, investigating the pain thresholds of each twin, obsessively curious as to which one would die first. Mengele was known for performing sexual experiments as well. His depravity seemed to know no bounds. Mengele used Nazi racial theory to justify experiments on Jews and Roma. Many people subjected to his investigations died from them – and in some, death was the intended outcome. He also made sick people sicker to find out what their pain limit would be.

Mengele had pursued experiments on Lisabelle at her bedside. On his orders, she had been forced to lie in the same bed in which terminally ill people had died from highly infectious diseases – from which none had recovered. Those filthy death beds had not been changed in months. For two weeks, Lisabelle had gone night after night from bed to bed, from one contagious sickness to another. Dr. Mengele wanted to see how contagious and deadly the diseases were and how the patients managed even when untreated. He did not care whether Lisabelle lived or died in the process. Anna, with her nursing experience, had monitored Lisabelle's progress for Mengele, while secretly giving her medication and food. Lisabelle's recovery from illness was thanks to Anna's care. That is why when Lisabelle got better, she was sent to work in Kanada, where many of the teenage inmates worked.

Lisabelle's job was to inspect clothing seams and suitcase linings in search of hidden valuables such as gemstones, money, and gold that may have been hidden there. Sometimes, Lisabelle would find photos tucked into the seams, and she would quietly weep for the families torn apart.

Lisabelle told Hetty and the group that there were buildings a mile long full of Jewish property looted by the Nazis. There were unimaginable riches hidden in garments, suitcases, and boxes, but eventually, everything was found and stolen from the rightful owners. There was also theft in those sheds, because German soldiers sometimes entered and took liquor, cigarettes, and jewelry before the workers registered the goods. It might have been the only place where that was possible, because there was just a short window of opportunity to take things before they had been recorded in the ledgers.

Anna Rosenthal had indeed helped Lisabelle escape Auschwitz. She had continually watched over her, managed to get her well, got her out of Mengele's evil hands, made sure she was put to work in a comparatively better environment, saw to it that she returned to the barracks and the camp, and oversaw that at the first possible opportunity, Lisabelle got on a train to Reichenbach.

Six entire months had gone by, and Lisabelle and her mother were reunited and stayed together from then on, under the protection of the ladies of the Philips group.

Lena was full of gratitude and admiration for Anna, who had managed to never forget her promise. Anna had snuck in to examine the order ledgers to find out where Hetty and Lena had been sent. The return of Lisabelle was proof to them all that there were still some good people in the world. Later, during the Nuremberg trials when Anna was accused and tried for treason, Lena traveled there to testify on Anna's behalf, and she was successfully acquitted.

30

FRITZ, JUNE 1945

WARTIME & POSTWAR AMSTERDAM

The Van Dykes explained to Fritz what they had witnessed in Amsterdam. They had seen the street raids firsthand. After the raids, they saw that homes of Jews had been sealed shut. Then they saw the seals broken. A hierarchy of officials had been given permission to confiscate all the possessions left behind. Hitler and his generals had first choice and gathered valuables like paintings, jewelry, artifacts, furs, crystal, diamonds, pearls, gold, and silver. Then the Dutch police were given entry and permission to take things they wanted as reward for helping catch Jews and the others who were to be extinguished. Succeeding levels of command continued to loot what was left, and after each group had chosen what they wanted, anything remaining was immediately removed by the Nazis and sold or put on containers and sent to Germany.

They had also witnessed a horrific drama on the street one day. The Nazis had caught a wanted Resistance man and shot him point-blank as he kneeled on the asphalt in the middle of the street. They forced him down to his knees with his hands behind his back and then shot him right in the forehead. The Van Dykes watched him topple over, his blood pooling in the street. The Nazis just left him lying there.

The women wanted now to prepare Fritz for the disappointments he would feel after returning to Benno's old place. They warned him that, all of the hidden items would probably be gone, though they wondered how anyone could justify going in and looting the homes of the deported.

Fleur said, "As soon as we had heard that you and Hetty had been taken by force, we went to your apartment to see for ourselves, and we saw that it had been sealed shut. No unauthorized people were allowed in. The entrance was totally taped shut with signs that this property was off-limits to everyone. Several buildings had been completely emptied."

Olivia said, "We had no idea where all of the tenants had gone, but we assumed they were at the Nazi headquarters. This time we were not so sure you both would be returning like you did after your first arrest. But according to our news source, no one was dying in extermination camps. They thought people were just missing and had been sent to work camps but would surely turn up again.

"Then one day in 1943, eyewitness accounts started coming in, and we heard of atrocities that we just could not believe. We could not picture what an extermination camp looked like and what happened there. We just couldn't fathom what we were hearing. It confirmed what you had heard back at the Resistance meeting the night before your wedding the year before.

"Later, we heard that the possessions of the Jews were sealed up in containers and sent on ships to Germany. The apartments were left bare. After a while, new people were assigned to these apartments. It was terribly unfair and outrageous but, you know, a street full of empty houses was haunting. When people started walking around in our neighborhood again, it became a little less disturbing here."

So it was true, Fritz thought, that many of the new residents knew that valuables were hidden in the walls and attics and had demolished property in search of them. Fleur was the one with a lump in her throat now. She had listened to Fritz's stories and felt overcome with guilt. "Were we not all responsible for the atrocities that took place here in the Netherlands? By turning our heads and ignoring the wrongdoing? Watching as neighborhoods were emptied without finding a way to stop them?"

Olivia continued telling him how life in Amsterdam in the two years that Fritz was absent had drastically changed. "Last winter was one of the coldest in history. Also, at that time, German soldiers started leaving their posts to go to the front lines or go AWOL. Who knows where they went? Their disappearance created stagnation of the supplies that had been coming into Holland and many of the needed provisions were no longer available."

The average citizen could not get or find food in the cities. Trains had stopped arriving altogether, in part because people had stolen so many railway ties for cooking fires and for warmth. The shortage of supplies had affected every household. Everything had stopped coming to Amsterdam; even with food stamps, there was nothing to buy. The temperature had dropped far below freezing, and 25,000 people died from illness, hunger, and cold.

"People were eating tulip bulbs to stay alive." Fleur gestured to the living room, and added: "You can see we had to burn all of our wooden furniture for warmth."

Fleur spoke of how, during the worst of the famine, people left hungry in the morning, taking a spoon along with them, hoping to find food somewhere, anywhere. Many people found scraps of food on the street by the open markets, which had dwindled down to barely anything. Or they would eat out of garbage cans behind the few hotels that had managed to stay afloat.

They told Fritz of the scarcity, the terror, and the hunger that had kept Amsterdam in its grip during the war years. Now, at the end of the war, nothing was available. They had to use coupons for buying clothes, and supplies of all kinds were rationed. Rubber was gone.

Tires were worn and unavailable even for bikes. It was strenuous to cycle even short distances on these makeshift bicycles. People biked kilometers into the countryside to buy and trade meat and vegetables straight from the farmers, usually in exchange for other things because most people had no money. Businesses sometimes had cars or trucks, but practically no one else did.

They would have to show their papers to the many Nazi soldiers stationed on bridges and at crossroads. With these delays, it could take hours to travel to the farmlands, and sometimes what they had just acquired, including makeshift wheelbarrows or bicycles, was stolen by armed bandits. People living in the cities lacked supplies more than in the countryside. Trading for supplies was all the people could do, and food stamps were used as currency. An economic crisis had paralyzed the country and money was scarce; one egg was a luxury item. Everyone came to know what real hunger was.

Olivia said, "When the German soldiers left, the country suffered from serious neglect. The Netherlands was in a dysfunctional and broken state. The southern regions had already been freed, but the rest of the country had a long wait before Amsterdam was liberated. Train transportation was still at a standstill. Government offices have only just reopened."

Sally had only recently told her family about the German soldier she had briefly fallen for. He had been a German clerk in Sally's office at the beginning of the war. He was a nice fellow, and she was attracted to him and had developed affectionate feelings for him. However, she had avoided mentioning this to anyone because she felt so bad about it. She had found out that he was appalled by the orders he had to comply with, and he shared Sally's sentiments. Even though she felt close to him, she knew that this affair had no future, and after several months she broke off the relationship. Ending the contact was far more difficult than she had expected. She cared for him, and she felt bad that all the German soldiers were considered evil. She also did not want to reject him harshly, so that he might have reason to dig up dirt on her. Imagine if he found out about her hidden Jewish background? But she also did not want to insult the Jews by undertaking a love relationship with an enemy soldier.

For Fleur, when the Allied Forces landed at Normandy in June 1944, it was a turning point for her. She and her boyfriend, Jan, had been planning to get married for a while. He had proposed at the beginning of the war. After the invasion, she was hoping to get the wedding plans underway; it had become an exceptionally long wait.

When Amsterdam was liberated on May 5, 1945, the joy was inconceivable. The Allied Forces paraded down the streets in rows of tanks. Everywhere, people lined the streets, laughing in happy celebration of the victory. Champagne and beer were everywhere. The Dutch were dancing in the streets along with the Canadians and Americans who had freed them. No one had ever seen such a happy, joyous crowd.

This festive liberation affected everyone. Relief was overflowing now that the war in Europe had finally come to an end. Hitler and his cohorts were dead, and the Germans had surrendered. The Nazi horror had lasted five years.

Later in the year, V-J Day, or victory over Japan Day, marked the official end of World War II, on August 14, 1945. Both Germany and Japan had both lost. There had been a triumph of good over evil. The world had won.

On April 4, the Ohrdruf concentration camp, a subcamp of Buchenwald, was the first of the Nazi concentration camps to be liberated by the US Army. None of the soldiers had expected to find the prisoners in such a terrible condition. Death and disease were everywhere. The guards had abandoned the camp, leaving the locked-in inmates to slowly starve to death or die from one of the diseases running rampant. Yet, that was not the worst of the conditions they found. Some prisoners had been forced to sleep on barbed wire, which had become embedded in their skin. These emaciated victims were unable to move, and the wounds caused them fatal abrasions that lice were feasting on. The prisoners had been living in barracks full of dead people, filth, and vermin. The rats nibbled at the corpses, yet the men were not fazed. The prisoners had been forced to live among the dead without proper sanitation for quite some time.

Most of the Allied soldiers who liberated the camp were so horrified at what they found that they just fell to their knees and wept. The Allies insisted that the high British and American commanding officers come to witness these atrocities for themselves. On April 12, Generals Eisenhower, Bradley, and Patton visited the camp and were appalled. Eisenhower quickly sent a cable to General Marshall in Washington: "...The visual evidence and the verbal testimony of starvation, cruelty and bestiality were so overpowering as to leave me a bit sick. In one room, where they were piled up 20 or 30 naked men, killed by starvation, George Patton would not even enter. He said that he would get sick if he did so. I made the visit deliberately, in order to be in a position to give first-hand evidence of these things if ever, in the future, there develops a tendency to charge these allegations merely to 'propaganda.'"

The Allied soldiers forced the Nazis who had been captured while fleeing, as well as the few Nazis who remained warm in trailers outside the camps, to clean up the mess they had left behind. It was grimy and repulsive in the camps, and the rats and other pests proved that. The Nazis whom the Allied officers interrogated claimed that there were no medical supplies available for prisoners; yet, the Allies had found ample sterile bandages, disinfectant materials, and medicines locked away on the premises – the Nazi soldiers had simply chosen not to help the prisoners.

In the last weeks of the war no food was available because the Nazi guards had hastily left their posts the moment they realized that the liberating allied armies were nearby. The prisoners were like the walking dead. Skeletons. Nazi soldiers and camp guards did not want to be captured or put on trial, so they had fled the scene.

Fritz had heard that villagers in some areas knew nothing about the concentration camps, even the ones right in their neighborhood. They must have smelled the scent of death, Fritz thought. The Allied officers, who had never witnessed anything so shocking, decided it was important to show it to these villagers. They were invited, actually required, to visit the camp site and see for themselves what had gone on inside; they would be firsthand witnesses to how their own countrymen had tortured and massacred millions of human beings. They would be confronted with the atrocities the Nazis had perpetrated.

Clad in fashionable attire, as if on a holiday excursion, some with fur coats and others wearing hats with veils and shiny boots, the unsuspecting visitors laughingly boarded a bus to visit a concentration camp where they received a tour. A growing discomfort surrounded them. They were led inside broken-down barracks with smashed windows, full of decaying bodies; they witnessed corpses piled up in the buildings and around the grounds. Sometimes a body that was not completely dead would move, and the villagers would shriek. The demeanor of these visitors changed dramatically, and they choked and gagged at the rotten stench of death.

To their astonishment, together with the Nazi soldiers, they were commanded to finish digging the abandoned mass graves and instructed to carry bodies to the gaping holes. It took them all afternoon. When the visitors boarded their bus for the return journey, they held handkerchiefs over their noses and mouths, coughing from the stench. Most were sobbing as they came face to face with how the naked and emaciated corpses had been treated. They would surely tell friends and family what they had seen. Knowing the truth was appalling and shocking, and Fritz daydreamed about the shock these visits had on the unsuspecting locals.

One by one, the camps were liberated with the fall of the Nazi regime. But, although the gates had swung open and the prisoners invited outside to be cared for, none of the prisoners had trusted the Allies at first. Fritz, and most other inmates, did not budge. Fritz did not believe that the war was truly over or that the new soldiers meant no harm. Fritz had not wanted to trust the invitation to step outside. They all thought that they might be mowed down by gunfire if they assembled outside the gates. The Allies who rescued Fritz had fed him, treated his wounds, and gained his trust. Then, inmates were given a small amount of money for travel. Because the European public transportation system was largely inoperable, the men left on foot wearing only rags, or with a small knapsack and their prison uniforms on their backs, like Fritz had. They all went in different directions. So many nationalities had been thrown together, and now each of them had to find a way to return to their homelands.

The Canadian and American allies had been kind. However, when the Russian troops arrived from the East, their need to take revenge on the Nazi regime incited a murderous killing spree. The Nazis had murdered entire villages of innocent civilians in Russia during the war. Farmers, their wives, and their children had all perished, murdered by the Nazi battalions. For the last two years of the war, one village every other day was demolished. The inhabitants were shot or burned to death, and then the entire area was plowed down and covered with dirt. It was as if the villagers and their village had never existed. Neighboring towns were astonished that a town could just vanish altogether. Families would not find a single remnant of their relatives left. That is why the Russians were obsessed with taking revenge on the Germans, killing anything that moved, whether it was civilians or military. They went on a raping and killing spree and murdered three million German and Austrian citizens as they traveled West to free more camps. Fritz had seen it with his own eyes.

He had spoken to a German woman who had been freed from the Bergen-Belsen concentration camp only to be raped by the Russians on her way home.

The Dutch were now using the vacated Dutch concentration camps to imprison Dutch traitors. Almost immediately, after May 5, collaborators were rounded up and incarcerated in the camps where they had kept the Jews during the war. There, they would await trial. These traitors and collaborators were shaved bald, as they had done to the Jews, and were made to do the walk of shame wherever they went. They had committed crimes and would be tried in the courts. Yet they would be treated far better than the Jews had ever been. The Jews had not committed any crime. The Jews had been judged and mistreated just for being born.

Many high-ranking Nazis managed to escape Europe in the early days after the war. They had planned their escape long before the actual defeat of Germany, and, in many cases, the Vatican assisted in the escape and provided new identities and maps to the escape routes in exchange for Jewish gold. Many war criminals ended up leading normal lives, most of them in Brazil, Chile, and Argentina. The Americans brought thousands of German Nazi scientists to the US at the end of the war who could assist them in developing nuclear weapons and in space exploration. It was called Operation Paperclip. This would not be uncovered for a few decades, but it would blemish the reputation of the Americans who considered the mad scientists worthy of studying. The war criminals were given new identities and paid jobs, and they were able to congregate with their fellow countrymen who were also treated extremely well. The horror continued because they also started new chapters of Nazism in the countries they fled to, to keep the ideology alive.

PART 5

DYING WORLDS

31

HETTY, JANUARY 1945

DEATH MARCHES

All of the women still remaining in the Philips group stayed together in Reichenbach for a total of six months.

The Russian Army blew up the train tracks around Reichenbach as they approached, which delayed the arrival of materials the women needed to continue working. The Nazis did not know what to do with these women with no work for them to do. Still, the bosses insisted that all prisoners remain working; so, when the supplies stopped arriving, they would walk to the Reichenbach factory every night despite having nothing to do, and would then be marched back to their barracks in the early morning.

The only option for the Nazis at that point was to empty the camps and outrun the Russian Allies, who were close by. But all of these women were slowing them down. As the tension grew, the Nazis took out their anger and anxiety on the inmates. There were still too many eyewitnesses to their cruelty – too many people who could prove the Nazis had committed unspeakable war crimes against humanity. Hitler wanted to eliminate them altogether, but what he didn't know was that Himmler needed them as a negotiating tool to make a deal with the Allies.

Himmler was the most fanatical Aryan race advocate of them all. He considered the Jews and Slavic people to be "human animals" with no value except for the labor they could provide. The totalitarian, extermination-crazy Himmler gave a lengthy 116-page speech on October 4, 1943, in which he openly expresses the intentions of the Nazi party: "If while building a tank ditch, 10,000 Russian women die from weakness or not, that interests me only insofar as the tank ditch is built for Germany." He told his SS Generals, "In front of you here, I want to refer explicitly to a very serious matter.... I mean here...the annihilation of the Jewish people.... Most of you will know what it means when 100 corpses lie side by side, or 500 or 1,000.... This page of glory in our history has never been written and will never be written.... We had the moral right; we were obligated to our people to kill this people which wanted to kill us." On top of that, he had a twisted notion that "good blood" could be salvaged by kidnapping Polish children with Aryan traits and placing them in German Aryan homes to be raised. Some 200,000 Polish children were abducted from their homes and transported to Germany.

By spring 1945 it had become clear that the Germans were losing the war. Himmler and many other of Hitler's deputies had been aware that Hitler's mental state had been deteriorating for some time and his military judgment was severely impaired. Hitler's generals were quite alarmed at the level of addiction to crystal meth Hitler had reached.

In April 1945, Himmler met with the Swedish Red Cross representative, Folke Bernadotte, in an attempt to negotiate peace with the Allies. He presented himself as the new provisional leader of Germany. During these negotiations, he promised to stop the mass extermination of Jews and vulnerable people at concentration camps. Ultimately, the Allies rejected Himmler's peace offer, not wishing to negotiate with a man who had committed war crimes.

However, just because the Jews would no longer be mass murdered in gas chambers, there were other ways to kill them. The SS understood that Himmler's word "evacuation" was code for "elimination." Himmler authorized eliminating the captives by starving them instead. No food was to be given during the Death Marches over the mountains or on transports.

One January night in 1945, instead of going to work, Hetty's group was called together to appear for a head count, after which they were moved by truck to a new place. This was an awful camp, where Hetty had been interned during her illness. It was a sub-camp not far from Reichenbach, where the temperatures were 30-35 degrees below zero. Just unimaginable. All of the windows in the camp's lavatory were broken. There were several inches of ice and icy water pooled on the floor, and open, damaged toilets, with no lighting. They were forced to wake up at 3:30 a.m. for the head count, which took an hour, during which they nearly froze to death. They were then forced to line up in columns of five people next to one another and told to start running over the icy paths back to the factory they had worked in before. Hetty's group, still primarily made up of the Philips women, were told that they were being chased by the Russians.

After staying at Camp Langenbielau for four weeks, on February 18, 1945, approximately 1,000 women inmates were evacuated on a death march as the Nazis fled the Russians. As usual, they needed to remain in rows of five, with just one hunk of bread each and nothing else. They were forced to walk on foot 120 kilometers (about 75 miles) over the Eulengebirge mountain ranges to Camp Trautenau in the mountains in the middle of winter, to Czechoslovakia. They were to work in a spinning factory, making thread for prison uniforms.

They walked 30 kilometers a day, either in huge, broken, wooden clogs or barefoot, in below-freezing temperatures. Most of them had diarrhea, and of course there was no warm food, nothing to drink, and all they could do was just walk for hours – then days. Climbing high over the mountains with only ice on the ground to eat, they ate mugs full of snow. The stomach pain and diarrhea continually got worse for everyone. But if someone paused or could not keep going, they were shot on the spot, without question and without emotion. Many just dropped dead by the wayside.

Hetty was somehow able to keep going. She wasn't sick, but at night she was so tired that she could not take one more step, and at one point she almost just let them shoot her.

Dottie did not even have the wooden clogs that some of the others still possessed and had to walk the entire 120 kilometers barefoot in the snow. The soles of her feet turned dark blue.

The incredible damage to their mental and physical health, as well as the exposure to the elements, was just too much for many. The dehumanization was the straw that broke the camel's back. Going against orders meant a bullet between the eyes, so they just walked on. They had seen so many dead people by that point that they didn't care any more. They couldn't. When night fell, the women slept in what seemed to have been a large barn, where they laid in cow and horse dung to keep warm. In the morning, the moment it got light, the Nazis forced them to get up. With nothing to wash with, nor anything at all to eat, they were again made to march on, arriving at Trautenau on the fifth day, filthy and exhausted.

At Trautenau, there were no barracks for them. They had to lie down between the machines to sleep, on a hard dirt floor. As usual, they were given no food; though, by that time, many were not interested in food at all. It took too much strength to eat. After five days working at the spinning mill, they were once again moved, in an attempt to evade the Russian forces.

The move occurred in the middle of a snowstorm. They were loaded onto an open cattle car, standing up, again given only one hunk of bread to sustain them throughout the journey. The train traveled for six days and nights in below-freezing weather. Hetty learned there how to sleep standing up, because there was no room to lie down crammed into a cattle car with 140 women. She knew better than to lie down, because if she did, she was likely to be trampled and would be dead in no time. Each morning many dead bodies were thrown out of the car. Because so many had died, there was eventually room to sit down.

Everyone was weak when they arrived at the Porta Westfalica camp, but it would be another three days before they got anything to eat. Hetty felt hungrier there than at any other time during the war. They had to walk long distances back and forth to the mountains each day to work in a factory situated deep underground. Although there was an elevator, they were not allowed to use it. They were made to climb over 200 meters down and up every day. This underground camp had been built in a salt mine, which was now full of machinery and various parts to make radios.

The women remained there until April 1, when they were again crammed together in cattle cars and sent to Beendorf. Another five days without food. When they arrived at Beendorf they were beaten with wooden sticks. The entire camp was teeming with lice.

On April 10, they were put on transport again, though they had no idea of their destination. Hetty learned that it was not the Russians now, but the Americans who were coming to free them and from whom they were running. This trip was the worst she had experienced, even worse than Auschwitz-Birkenau. The train zigzagged through the Lüneburgerheide, which lies between Hamburg and Berlin. They were all starved, and many had gone mad.

The transport from Beendorf took another five days and was huge, including 3,000 women and 2,000 men. Again, there was no food. They received nothing for days, and they kept saying to one another, "They have to give us something." They were in a cattle car populated with a mix of Polish women, German criminals, and Roma women.

The train finally came to a standstill outside of Bergen-Belsen. Bergen-Belsen did not have a gas chamber. Dottie had heard that her sister was in Bergen-Belsen, and she hoped she might yet be alive and that she could see her. Stretching their legs outside the cattle cars, they were given some soup. The first of anything they had eaten in days.

A few prisoners from the camp were assisting in handing out what little rations there were, and Dottie happened to ask one of them if he knew her sister. Amazingly, he did! Because her sister had studied in Paris and was fluent in French, she had become an interpreter for the Greek community in the camp. The educated Greeks spoke French, so her skills were needed, and it was why she was known there. Still, of the many thousands of people there, Dottie was amazed this person knew her, and that she was still alive.

Ultimately, however, they were refused entry because the camp was completely full. It had ended up being a lucky break for the Philips women, because Bergen-Belsen was currently dealing with an outbreak of typhoid fever. Tens of thousands of people had died there from starvation and illness.

So they were sent away yet again. This time, the train came to a stop in a place called Lüneburger-Heide in northern Germany, not far from Bergen-Belsen. They remained there for many days, hearing the roar of the battlefields in all directions. At regular intervals a Nazi stood with a gun and a dog like a roadblock so that nobody would try to run for it. They all simply sat in a meadow doing nothing during the day, with no food, without anything. Hetty was relieved that at least they were outside, not stuffed into one of the cattle cars. The Nazis had no idea what to do with them, their enemies closing in on all sides, with Russians coming from the east and the Allied Forces from the west. The Nazis just sat in their train compartments with food, eating and waiting. But there was nothing for the prisoners. The Nazis wanted them to die. They had no orders to shoot anyone, so they starved them instead, and many more lives were lost. The prisoners hung on there for seven or eight days. Each night they had to return to the cattle car. They had not been given any coats or blankets, despite it being February in northern Europe.

Besides having to battle the elements, fearing the Germans, the Russians, the bombing, and the starvation, they then also became dreadfully afraid of the Roma gypsies on board the train.

A group of Roma women had joined Hetty's cattle car. One day when they were without work and there was no food, she witnessed two Roma start a fire with two rocks. They fetched a dead, wretched body from the open cattle car, held a slice of thigh over an open flame, then started to eat it. Apparently, one of them had a knife. That was Hetty and Dottie's first and only encounter with cannibalism. Dottie did not think she would have ever thought of doing that, but the scent of meat cooking drove them both mad. It was the first time Hetty realized she could be hungry again. Yet she remained quiet and suffered in silence. She felt there was no way that these very self-reliant but aggressive women would have shared anything with her anyway.

The Nazis must have received orders to move yet again, so the prisoners were ordered onto the train once more. Hetty was standing glued next to another woman, whom she observed wriggling out of her underpants right there in front of her. Hetty asked the woman what she was doing. She said she had had those underpants on for three weeks and they were so soiled that she did not want to wear them anymore. Hetty asked her if she could have them, and the woman said yes. Hetty was pleased, as she had not worn any underwear for some time and was freezing cold. Although it took some effort, she slowly squirmed into them as best she could in those cramped conditions.

Only moments later, a heated discussion erupted between a gypsy Roma and the women who had just given Hetty her underwear. Everyone was at their wits' end as more people joined in the argument, which became more and more heated. A female guard grabbed the woman who had just given Hetty her underwear and clubbed her to death right before Hetty's eyes. Hetty watched in horror as the woman's blood squirted in all directions, after which her body was unceremoniously thrown from the moving train. Hetty thought to herself that even if she lived to be 100 years old, she would never forget seeing that. What was worse is that she would never forget how seeing that made her feel. Then the guard turned to Hetty, and in a low voice, she whispered a few words of advice in her ear.

Not long after that, one of the Roma women attacked Hetty. She put two fists in Hetty's short hair, twisted and tangled it thereby pulling her every which way. She mumbled something about how Hetty had gotten special treatment by the guard. Hetty was repeatedly kicked and beaten over the head with a pipe and was not able to protect herself. Hetty thought the woman must have been jealous of the protection she had gotten from the guard. Perhaps the guard thought she was a child, being so small and delicate. Hetty was terrified she might die at the hands of yet another enemy. She would later say about it, "Strangely, though the Roma gypsy asking her buddies to finish me off, in which case I would have been trampled to death, they resisted." Hetty pushed herself up and started screaming so loudly that she was transformed into a madwoman, clawing and resisting with every ounce of power she had left. She could do nothing but scream and attempt to manage the pain she was feeling with each blow, each kick. After a few moments the others held the Roma woman back, forcing her to let Hetty go.

Eventually they arrived at Hamburg Eidelstedt after another ten days without food or water. It was yet another horrific camp. By then the last of the Philips group were in a terrible state, covered in lice and madly scratching their itchy skin. Nonetheless they were put to work there.

Dottie and Hetty had been given the job to remove the dead every morning. Together, they carried the corpses over to add them to one of the many piles of bodies stacked all around. It was up to them to decide who was dead and who was still alive.

32

FRITZ, JUNE 1945

THE RESISTANCE AT WORK

Each day, Fritz would spend hours talking with the Van Dykes. They were very willing listeners. They shook their heads every time something was said that was too awful to comprehend. The women were truly empathetic about what had happened to Fritz. Even though they had seen some horrors on the streets of Amsterdam themselves; those were nothing compared to what they were hearing from this eyewitness and trusted friend. They clearly noticed that Fritz would just not believe that he would not see Hetty ever again. The three women were unfortunately less sure about that than Fritz was, and they worried that he would die of a broken heart if he had no closure about her whereabouts. The women feared that there would never be a justice powerful enough to fill the void and sorrow that loss of family had caused. Would anyone ever get the needed closure knowing that the inflicted suffering was intentional? Those civilians who died during this war were not casualties of war. These dead were the targeted civilians, considered the enemy of mankind, at least of the Aryan race, and nothing could justify what had happened and to what extent. What had been inflicted on Fritz and had broken so many millions of families would surely leave enormous scars on the human race for decades to come. These conversations were extremely important, even though Fritz had pledged to himself to not relive any of it ever again. Though emotionally exhausting, speaking about what had happened was illuminating for them all.

During a pause in their exchanges, there came a knock at the door. It was Fritz's old Resistance buddy, Stan Davids. Stan had helped many people during the war, supplying them with forged documents and helping find them hiding places for families and children. Fritz was elated to see him, knowing he had just come out of hiding. This was a momentous occasion indeed. Stan was the sole survivor of his team of Resistance members, both Jewish and non-Jewish. All the others had been betrayed, captured, and executed.

As Stan sat with them and had tea, he told Fritz and the Van Dykes how nurses at the day-care center across the street from the Nazi headquarters in Amsterdam had been ordered to take children from the arms of the parents gathered in one building and bring them to another while the parents awaited results of the selection by the Gestapo.

The enemy's intention was to separate families and send them to their deaths, alone, and without each other. Stan related how there was a short window of opportunity for saving some of the small children and placing them in the care of willing strangers who would keep them safe in protective custody until their parents returned.

These nurses worked together with the Resistance to smuggle children out of Amsterdam and bring them to safe places in the countryside. A Resistance worker living in that region had been able to enlist the help of farmers. Usually, a host family knew just one Resistance worker. That worker recruited the farmer, who was willing to hide Jewish people. Sometimes only babies and younger children were welcome, because older children would stand out, and the host family might receive unwanted attention. In most cases, the parents of these hidden children, who had been arrested and processed at the Hollandse Schouwburg, would never see their children again.

The Resistance had managed to find hiding places for at least 600 children through the daycare center, most of whom had survived. It was a very risky operation because it occurred right in front of the Nazi headquarters. Each time a tram stopped at the little tram shelter in front of their door, the Nazis' view of the street would be obscured for a few moments. While the tram would wait for passengers to get off and on, the Nazis couldn't see who was boarding or leaving on the far side of the tram, the tram itself blocking the view of the entrance. Through the tram window, only the top half of the nurses clad in overcoats could be seen boarding. That childcare service, whose directive was to separate and destroy families, was actually helping to saving them.

"It was a very risky business," Stan said, "smuggling the children out of the daycare center. On cue, the nurses boarded the trams, the little children hidden underneath their long coats." He was still sad that he was not able to have helped more. When his cover was finally blown, he was blacklisted, and he had gone into hiding.

"It was sad to see the bewildered faces of the children who went along quietly, only because their parents had promised to be back the very next morning when the kids woke up," Stan said. "The parents had needed to lie, of course, because they wanted their children to go peacefully with these strangers, without making a scene that might endanger them and others. All of those parents really thought they might be able to pick their children up the next day, or at least soon thereafter."

But most of the birth parents were sent far, far away the next day to some remote extermination camp somewhere in eastern Europe and were gassed there, never to return.

The parents were given only moments to decide whether they wanted their children hidden and saved, or whether they would risk taking them along on the journey ahead of them. Not everyone assumed that going on transport meant death, but many suspected it and wanted their children to have a future, even if meant never seeing them again.

The nurses would enter the headquarters where the parents were waiting for their papers to be reviewed, walk up to them, look them in the eyes, and whisper, "You have one minute to decide whether you agree to entrust me with your child. I will hide your son with good people and keep him safe. If not, then your boy can go with you, but beware, he can be taken from you at any time and subjected to life-threatening danger – or killed. I will get all your information next time I come in and tell you where you can pick up your son upon your return."

"Don't think that the parents were abandoning their kids," Stan said. "They just wanted them to survive and to have a good life. It took courage to give their child to strangers and trust anyone promising to care for them in such a sadistic war. Those parents deserve the utmost praise for having saved their children from suffering and perhaps death."

The children received new identities, and many were instructed to learn the Christian "Lord's Prayer" in case of a raid or being questioning by an enemy soldier, a traitor, or a collaborator. Because of this, the young kids started believing that they were Christians. This was a good thing in the eyes of the gentile hosting families. If the kids started believing they were not Jewish, everyone would be safer. Hiding Jews was punishable by death, so many people could not be trusted. Even within a household, a farmer's child could resent the risk his parents were taking with their lives. Also, familiar friends of a farmer needed a reasonable explanation for the sudden appearance of another child in the household, and those lies were often not believed. Anyone, even your neighbor, could be working with the enemy. The nurses were risking their lives, too. They had to keep everything quiet. The day-care director, along with all of the staff, had managed to keep their activities a secret while they deceived the Nazis, and they were never caught.

"How could people rationalize letting their own Jewish friends be violated, abused, and victimized, let alone subject them to such cruelty, betray them, and help murder them?" Sally asked.

Fleur said, "It was as if everyone had been under a spell; as though no Jew was expected to survive or come back to stake a claim to their children, property, cash, or any of their belongings."

No collaborator seemed to feel any remorse for their greed, for betraying the hideouts of Jews, and assisting in their death. And no one was prepared to give anything back when the original owners did, against all odds, miraculously return.

Fritz had no answer to explain how normal people could do to babies the unspeakable things that he had witnessed. That is when Olivia said, "You combat hate by being as kind as you can be to others, even when you don't understand their motives."

Stan said, "All of what was put into motion to annihilate the Jews was once just an idea in somebody's head, in Hitler's head, in his general's heads. Someone deranged and delusional had once conceived of it. We, as Resistance workers, had to find out what the plan was, and we had spies in place, but it took some time to figure out what their strategy and purpose was exactly. We, as citizens, understand how some mortals try to justify their deeds. But now that we know how to detect madness better, we know what we are up against, and we will never let it happen again. We learned that the Germans really believed they were a special race, and all other people could never measure up to them, had no value, and, therefore, should not be alive. The Nazis had had six years to prepare."

Stan told them how Hitler's doctor had been given a lab to create a drug to enhance his troops' endurance during warfare. It was called Pervitin, and although it kept the soldiers active for four days and nights without the need for sleep or food, it ended up killing many later on. Hitler ordered truckloads of it to be brought to battlefields and forced the battalions to ingest these drugs on a regular basis. They became killing machines, and their behavior became beastly. Hitler's doctor (who was also his drug dealer) spent the last winter of the war in a bunker with Hitler and was not allowed to leave his side because Hitler had become addicted to speed and needed his daily fix.

Not only Jews, but more than 70,000 patients with physical or mental health problems, including children, were murdered at Auschwitz. Physically and mentally impaired people were all systematically eliminated, because of the corrupt and unethical practices of the entire psychiatric system run by the Nazis. Germany required that doctors and nurses help betray Jews. More than 400,000 medical personnel admitted to being complicit in the genocide. Later, they claimed that they were forced to assist in the murders. This was done in secret and only recently became known.

"We can expect political change and revenge thinking to come about in the future, because the sorrow and grief will infect all of our lives, and as humans, we must prevent such ideology from ever entering our lives again. I pray that the coward Nazi leaders are held accountable for these crimes."

Fritz shook his head slowly. "The Nazis' dreadful lies served their cause, and their propaganda was effective. The big lie was blaming the innocent Jews, so we would be perceived as criminals." The concept of the big lie had been introduced by Hitler in his book, *Mein Kampf*. It was later propelled by Joseph Goebbels, his right-hand propaganda man. Such a gross distortion or misrepresentation of the truth causes most people to believe that nobody would possibly make up such a huge lie. And if they keep repeating it, people eventually believe it.

Stan said, "Their propaganda led to engaging large groups to participate, acquire funding, and get the German public all riled up. The masses went along when Germany attacked Poland in September 1939, because the groundwork had already been set. By then, their soldiers had been trained. They had already infiltrated businesses and schemed behind neighbors' backs. Employees, employers, co-workers, even family members might be scheming. In reality, many soldiers were dressed in plain clothes. We never suspected anything. Their minds had been poisoned by false news and they were influencing others. These soldiers did exactly what was asked of them because they believed the lies."

Stan's visit had left them all sad, but, at the same time, hopeful that the end of the war also signified the end of hatred. But would it?

Olivia said, "The Resistance expanded their network of people willing to hide Jews. Even though the risks were great, many acted selflessly. Most who took those risks and showed mercy to the Jews remained anonymous. I know of families that refused to comply and risked hiding Jews but never wanted their acts of bravery praised or rewarded. It was the right thing to do; it was the humane thing to do!"

Some families in the center of town had servants' quarters in the "back houses" of canal homes, which they could use for hiding Jews. Some homes were even large enough for small families to hide. Centuries before, wealthy merchants had built those canal houses. Some had long corridors connecting them to neighbors, with secret passageways suitable for fleeing, accessible by the kitchen or storage area. From the street, no one could imagine that there were large spaces behind the houses; the greenery and tall trees hid them. Most of these were disguised as bakeries and shops, but people were living in them during the war. Normal families hid both Jews and Resistance workers.

Local residents and tenants also created hiding places that were impossible for Nazi raiders to find. For instance, space in an empty upright piano could be made for one person to hide. Another useful space for one was created behind a blind wall in a utility closet. Then there was the crawl space between floors, with a ventilation screen as the entrance way. If there was a raid, there would be just a few moments to scramble to the hiding places – and if no sounds were made, no one sneezed, and no baby cried, these spaces saved lives.

Fake walls with mirrors on them were built to conceal hidden closets. Empty spaces behind walls became hiding places, and some people lived underneath staircases, behind gas heaters, or in a secret annex behind a bookcase, as in the case of the 13-year-old Anne Frank. She and seven others were ultimately betrayed. It was her father, Otto Frank, whom Fritz had known at Auschwitz.

33

HETTY, APRIL-MAY 1945

FREEDOM TO HEAL

Hetty and the few of her fellow prisoners remaining alive were ordered to board the cattle cars and were put on transport yet again, as bombs fell all around them. The train passed by Dresden right after it was bombed. They could see the destruction and flames spreading all over. Then, the train stalled, and they all had to get out. Standing on a hill overlooking the city, they were now able to see the extent of the destruction. Although the Allies were now near, Hetty and the others were still captive. They slept in barracks near Hamburg that night.

On April 29, those remaining were slowly dying; but the next day they heard that Hitler and some of the top men in his regime had committed suicide. It is so terribly sad that, even after the war officially ended, many of the Philips women would never make it home again.

On May 1 they were beaten out of the barracks once more with clubs and forced to board trains again. It was the first time Hetty had seen hay on the floor of the wagon, and it made her somehow hopeful, sensing that something had changed. The train ran along a ridge, from which they could see that Hamburg, the largest port city of Northern Germany and a very important location for the Nazi's war effort, had been completely destroyed. This single picture, the view Hetty saw of a dismantled, bombed Hamburg would always remain in Hetty's mind as a twisted symbol of freedom. There was no color to be seen, anywhere. There was only an ashy-gray, no-man's-land, the Allies' colorless signature of destruction. A signal of freedom and of hope at the same time. She was relieved but felt no joy.

After two days and nights in the train, again without food, they at last arrived at the Red Cross station at Padborg, a Danish town on the border with Germany. It was there that they realized they were now in Allied hands; but their lives were still not safe, because later, they heard that there could have been an entirely different ending to this untold story. It is because of the decision of one man, the train engineer who disobeyed his orders by the SS to derail the train and let it run into the Elbe River outside Hamburg. "Just let the evidence drown" were his instructions. Hetty and the others had already suspected that they might not make it to freedom because they did not know where the train was headed. What they did know is that the end was near. Their stamina was shattered. They did not know that the capitol of Germany, Berlin, had suffered irreparable ruin due to Hitler's egotistical denial to negotiate terms of surrender. He had held his ground that he would not surrender, and, instead, sacrificed thousands of Berlin residents in favor of his own madness. He was dead in his bunker on April 30, along with a few other of the elite German generals under his command. Hitler and others had left his own country in ruins, taking cowardly precautions for himself. Only then, on the day of his death, had he married his mistress, Eva Braun, and together they united in death. They would all swallow cyanide and die, rather than face the consequences of the evil they had ignited in the world. They were in the hands of the devil until the end, still wanting to destroy all of the captives, because if key witnesses of genocide survived, they would tell the world what had been done to them and would ruin his reputation for making Germany great again.

The survivors were living proof of the atrocious crimes the Nazis had committed. They would disgrace the Nazis and the German people. Hitler's failure would run very deep. The eyewitnesses who survived were the ones now in command and of whom the Nazis were afraid. The living evidence must be destroyed, and Germany's reputation must not be damaged for a second time, for the second world war that they had started and lost. Hetty's story would one day be a marker in the hallmark of history because her survival is no less than miraculous.

Everyone who saw the survivors arriving in Denmark could not believe their eyes. Many of those who remained looked half dead, unable to walk, to move, were unbelievably skinny, with grave wounds all over their bodies, covered with lice and other parasites. But they made it. The unsung hero, that train engineer who brought them to Denmark, was an angel whom Hetty vowed to always remember. Hetty and her group of friends, Lena, Lisabelle, Martha, Dottie, and others, were given a second chance at life because of him. Never underestimate the power of what one person, you, can do when you do the right thing.

There was no celebration for them, no parades, no fireworks, no champagne for these half dead people. Only the knowledge of their freedom. When Hetty arrived in Denmark, she thought that it truly was the beginning of something special. She felt elated that she had been spared. She felt as if divine intervention had brought her back from the dead to live as a free person once again. Most of all she had kept her promise to Fritz; she had made it! She was alive! However, they were still very close to death. If they had been exposed to any more of the brutal conditions, Hetty thought, none of them would have made it. All they had to do was keep living, keep breathing, keep hoping – just a few more seconds, hours, and days. Hetty smiled at the thought of her Memory Place, and it was there that she told Fritz she was alive. Then she cried.

Crown Prince Frédérik of Denmark came to greet them at Padborg. Hetty and the others could not believe their eyes when they saw stretchers, toilets, piles of bandages, and other medical articles from the outside world.

Then came that incredible moment, as if a spell had been broken, when the SS actually waved goodbye to them and said *Auf Wiedersehen*. The SS stayed behind as Hetty and the others traveled on into Denmark. The Danes had climbed onto the train with large banners to welcome them. Even though the survivors looked dreadful, smelled like cow dung, and were near death, the Danes smiled and waved. Hetty was amazed at being shown a kind of decency that she had never expected to see again. They had all become so conditioned to mistreatment that kindness seemed bizarre.

On May 8, with the capitulation of Germany and the Axis powers – including the deaths of Adolf Hitler and the Italian dictator Benito Mussolini – World War II in Europe was officially declared over. Hetty did not yet feel in a position to rejoice, because in the days and weeks that followed, they saw many more die, and they realized their own lives were hanging by a thread. Although they had survived until liberation day, many could never rejoice at all. They never attended any celebrations, and they witnessed more suffering while they tried to recover. Japan had not yet capitulated and was still causing havoc and death in Asia.

Once in Denmark, they were handed over to the Red Cross, who took care of them. The first thing the aid workers did was give them food; but many of them were too weak to digest it. The medical staff had never experienced people in such an emaciated state. Many were so weak that even eating bowls of warm porridge made them sick, so sick that some died from what has become known as "refeeding syndrome." This became an acute problem, caused by the lack of knowledge needed to treat the survivors properly. The Red Cross admitted that they had never seen anything comparable to the survivors' physical devastation, and they had no real knowledge of what foods to give them and in what quantities. Their bodies had been so abused that they could not tolerate anything at first. The diet was then adjusted and gradually administered, and they eventually started gaining weight again.

For at least two whole years, the victims had needed to wash themselves with cold water and no soap, and their skin by now felt like parchment paper, as though it were made of thin leather. It did not feel like normal skin feels. As well as all the dirt, they had had bedbugs and insects of all types to deal with. The bugs left deep hollow sores all over their body that couldn't heal because there was no way to treat them. No medication had ever been available to them.

Some former prisoners were just skin and bones, and others, like Dottie, were all bloated. She might have looked better than those who were skin and bones, but she was just as weak, with edema all over. The only medical thing in that whole time that Dottie had done was to have an infected tooth pulled with a pair of pliers by one of the sanitation men. No anesthetic; just sitting on a chair. It took one minute. Nobody had ever dared complain about their condition unless absolutely necessary. There were people who had appendicitis, for example, who just had to go for help. But the help usually was either being operated on without anesthetics or no help at all. Most of those having acute emergencies never returned from the operating room.

While in the care of the Red Cross, Hetty suffered from mild stomach cramps, but she was otherwise able to eat, mostly because of the relief – the possible end of the pain and deprivation. It was a miracle, and they called her an "old trooper." Her lungs were X-rayed and found to be healthy.

From there, she and the Philips women went by boat to Malmö, Sweden, arriving at a refugee camp. The first thing the Swedes did was relieve the survivors of their filthy attire. They took those pale stained dresses, full of bugs and filth and burned them. That was their liberation. When they were given the opportunity to shower, old fears surfaced, and they were reluctant to trust even these kind liberators. Their heads were washed with nice-smelling shampoo, after which they were powdered for lice removal. Now that they were clean, the women felt almost whole again. They weren't itching anymore, for the first time in years.

They were then brought to a school where they met up with other Dutch survivors, at which they remained in quarantine for six weeks. They were told that there was no way of getting back to the Netherlands for six months because so many of the railways and other forms of transport were still under repair. The Netherlands was also lacking in countless necessities after what was known as the "Hunger Winter"; everything had to be rebuilt and restocked.

In Malmö, the Swedish doctors took care of the women, covering themselves completely, protected from head to toe, including gloves. Many people had typhoid fever, which is very contagious. They were given medication, but often the wrong medicines, or the dosages were too strong for their weakened bodies to tolerate.

The Swedish Red Cross also provided them with a comb, a brush, and a towel, things none of them had owned since they had been sent to the camps. They had had absolutely nothing to their names.

Despite having to go easy on the food at first, Hetty often misbehaved, going berserk eating sweets and everything else under the sun because it was all so delicious! Every day, she and Dottie would eat candy, herring and sardines, waffles, even kladdkaka, a Swedish sticky chocolate cake. It was no surprise she was regaining weight; the delicacies kept coming and were well prepared and irresistible.

Each of the survivors was introduced to a volunteer host who helped them in any way they could. The host took them sightseeing, helped them fill out required papers, translated letters of importance, and sent telegrams. The survivors were also given stationery and pens so they could write to their families abroad. The host took them shopping, bought them clothes, treated them to meals, took them on tours, and interpreted interviews with the Swedish authorities, as well as helped them apply for new identity papers and passports because they would not be able to travel without them.

Perhaps because Sweden had managed to stay neutral during the war, Hetty felt more in shock here, where no war had taken place, than when she made the shift from normal life to camp life. In part, because she had been isolated from anything resembling normal life for two years. In Sweden, everything was available, fashionable, and attractive. The boulevards were lit up, and there was no trace of the nightmarish existence they had lived through, in stark contrast to the deathly assaults they had endured on a daily basis. Hetty could finally start relaxing now.

She was more than sad, however, to have witnessed such an evil side of humanity. It was like living in a hostile universe, cut off from kindness, love, and care. Being deprived of family support and subjected to hatred, humiliation and starvation had shown her the depth of the depravity a human is capable of. Under the Nazis' grand display of egotistical genius lurked an absence of humanity and confidence, because, in fact, they were an insecure lot that hated mankind as it was, which implies that they hated themselves too. It was an almost unbelievable drama when she thought about it. Hetty concluded that surviving it was the most unbelievable plot of all. She was determined to find Fritz and tell her story to him and to the world, because everyone deserves to know.

She knew she was going to need to stay in Sweden for six full months, but that was no punishment. She now met the angelic side of humanity daily, a much-needed experience for restoring her faith in the goodness of humankind.

34

FRITZ, JUNE 1945

FINALLY REWARDED

Fritz had written to the consulates of neighboring countries in search of Hetty. He also wrote to every person and organization he could think of who might help him find her – the World Jewish Congress, furriers in London, and embassies in Sweden.

By nightfall each day, he felt weak and tired; he still needed time to recover. Some evenings he was not able to tell the stories of the camps; he would retire early, too exhausted to talk to anyone. Luckily, the Van Dykes understood and let him be. They could see that his search was weighing heavily on him, in addition to grieving the loss of his own family and so much more.

He also had to reconcile his increasing disappointment each time he came back empty-handed from the Red Cross. But there were good things happening, too, and during the day he often now found himself to be more cheerful.

One night in his room he lit a candle and prayed, saying goodbye to all those who would never return, saying farewells to all the lost souls who had not been as fortunate as he had been. He also gave thanks for making it alive through the most harrowing period of human history ever known, one that he would never truly understand. Included in this ritual was mention of all those who had died alone, such as the living skeletons most prisoners had become – who had surely never returned home. Fritz had no idea how his own lost loved ones had perished, and so he silently saluted all those who had died in solitude who were left to rot in unmarked graves. He prayed for and mourned close family members, like Uncle Benno, and not knowing whether Hans or Martin Golden would ever return. He also took a little time to voice yet again his prayer that he would soon hear from Hetty. She would surely be looking for him.

Now that he was on the road to recovery, he sometimes asked himself: *Why did I survive? Why me?* Though not a lot was known about this at the time, Fritz would later come to know about survivor's guilt and post-traumatic stress disorder, a condition triggered by a terrifying event or events, causing flashbacks, nightmares, severe anxiety, and other physical manifestations. All of his experiences had become firmly lodged in his mind, and it had a disturbing effect on him for the rest of his life.

Lying there in bed, exhausted, a satisfying answer to those questions suddenly arose and interrupted his despair: *I know why I survived. Only an eyewitness will be believed. The following generations will hear and believe from the mouth of someone who knew such despair, and who saw what happened. The coming generations, across the globe – all must know.*

Fritz did not know whether he was closer to finding Hetty or not. He planned to write to Aunt Rosalie in America that very afternoon, after coming back from doing his rounds. He had not yet met any of Hetty's American family, and he wanted to introduce himself. He hoped that Rosalie might have heard from Hetty and know her whereabouts so she could send him her address.

He went out to run some errands and visit the Red Cross offices like every other day for weeks, to quiz them about the next step in the process of locating people. The problem was that all of Europe was in an uproar. The postal service was overwhelmed. Everywhere, people were in search of missing persons. There were millions of them trying to reach home, and many camp survivors were using the postal service to contact others and ask for money. The need to communicate was enormous. It had grown far beyond the capacity of the postal system.

Supplies were universally low, and trains were not yet running everywhere. Life had slowed dramatically, due in part to all the damage that both the Nazis and the Allies had inflicted on much of Europe during the conflict. And because the post was also dependent on trains, almost nothing was delivered on time. The mail was vital for helping stranded survivors buy even simple necessities such as clothes and shoes. It would take some time, and a lot of funding and labor, before everything was up and functional again. The telegraph service was equally overwhelmed. Outdated news arrived too late in all of postwar Europe.

Everyone had to be patient. And although the authorities were trying to improve conditions as quickly as possible – it was still frustrating and exhausting. Everyone's patience had worn thin after five years of war, and now they were being told to keep being patient a while longer. They were going crazy waiting for news of their loved ones. A letter dated May 20 might arrive a few weeks earlier than a letter dated May 10.

The fastest way to get messages sent was a one-sentence telegram; however, because each letter of every word was paid for separately, it was expensive. There were long lines down the street of people waiting to send telegrams – a familiar scene for Fritz.

Depending on which countries were involved, communication via post was limited to postcards. Sending packages was limited, and in some regions even banned. All these factors went through Fritz's mind as he left Olivia's home that afternoon to do his usual rounds, and he was rethinking how to approach the problem of finding Hetty.

He had just left the house when the doorbell rang. Olivia found a young soldier in American uniform standing on their doorstep. He started to speak in Dutch, but with a strong American accent. "My name is Harald Wolf. I live in the United States and am currently stationed here. I am a relative of Hetty Golden and her aunt Rosalie in New York. Rosalie asked me to check in on you. She sent me here to look for Hetty and Fritz Frankel, who have been off the radar since leaving Camp Vught in March last year." Then he asked, "Have you heard from either of them?" Olivia brightened and said, "Yes, I have. Fritz is staying here with us, but he is not at home now. Come in, come in, have a cup of tea, wait a bit, and perhaps Fritz will be back soon."

Harald asked a lot of questions, and they conversed for some time. He also heard from Olivia that Hetty had not yet surfaced, which was why Fritz was out searching for her daily. Harald was thrilled and, in a hurry to pass the good news on to Rosalie, decided to leave before seeing Fritz. He thanked Olivia, and in obvious excitement told her he would send the good news through the Military Mail Service which was much more efficient than by 'snail mail'.

The next day, June 25, Fritz finally saw a name on the Red Cross listing that made his mind whirl with excitement. He did not doubt for a second that the name he saw on the list of camp survivors was Hetty's, although the first name did not match. He had found the name: "Betty Frankel-Golden," among the living. The name was listed as part of the Philips group, which had been liberated in Denmark and then brought to Sweden. *Yes!* Fritz thought, and he knew instantly that this was Hetty. He stood still for long moments, trying to absorb this wonderful news.

With his head in the clouds, he barely saw anything or anyone on the streets as he walked toward home. He felt dazed and lightheaded, in a kind of shock all the way to the Van Dyke's. He couldn't wait to share with them that he had found her.

At the house he found the women in the kitchen preparing a meal and chatting. As he stood in the kitchen doorway, leaning against the door frame and gazing at them with a peculiar look on his face, they could see that something had changed. He raised his eyebrows and beamed at them with a crooked grin. Without saying anything at all, they knew that he had found Hetty at last. They all rejoiced together at this unforgettable day. This memorable moment. They hugged one another and danced together in a circle, rejoicing out loud for a few moments, until Fritz went completely quiet and had to excuse himself. The chatter and excitement in the kitchen were just too much; he was on the verge of sobbing and needed to process it all.

With a dishtowel in her hands, Olivia walked Fritz to the stairs and said to him, "Take your time. Now we pray. Let her be well." As Fritz climbed the stairs, he heard the women talking, then their voices wavered, then they began to cry as well. At last, he felt some of his anxiety dissipate, and his shoulders relaxed. So many emotions occurred at once. His feelings of hope had been rewarded. Everything that he had held onto for so long, ever since losing track of Hetty in March 1944, seemed now resolved. Fritz walked unsteadily into his attic room, sat down on his bed, and put his head in his hands. Tears of joy streamed down his cheeks and his body shook. He was thankful for The Memory Place, knowing that the hope he had cultivated there had rewarded him today. He had found her; she was alive.

PART 6

LETTERS ACROSS THE WORLD

35

FRITZ, JUNE 1945

LETTERS FROM AMSTERDAM TO THE US AND BACK

After returning from finding Hetty's misspelled name on the Red Cross list, Fritz wrote to Rosalie in America for the first time. He expressed his thanks to her for sending Harald Wolf and explained that he had been out searching for Hetty every day since his return from Auschwitz.

Dear Auntie Rosalie,

A few weeks ago, we heard a broadcast on Swedish radio that said many Dutch women in the Philips group were being held in a Dutch refugee camp in Sweden. I almost did not dare hope that she was among them. And then just today I saw her name on a Red Cross survivor's list. Would you be so kind as to let me know immediately, preferably by telegram, where she is, if you have heard from her? Also, please send me her address if you know it... Looking forward to meeting you and much love from,

Fritz

Rosalie responded:

Dear Fritz,

Hetty is indeed alive and has surfaced. She is with the Philips group in Malmö. You just can't imagine how I felt when I received the letter from Harald announcing that you are home with the Van Dykes. I thought my heart would just burst because I was so happy for Hetty. I have already received a few telegrams and letters from her, and every time she asks only about you and if I would help her find you as quickly as possible. I sent a telegram to her right away, and she immediately sent one back. Her closing words were "Tell Fritz about me." Now you have the assurance that you both are alive and can look forward to reuniting as soon as possible. And what a reunion that will be!

Much love from, Rosalie

36

LETTERS FROM MALMÖ TO AMSTERDAM & NEW YORK

Only days after Fritz sent his letter to Rosalie asking if she knew of Hetty's whereabouts, the Van Dykes received a letter from Hetty that had been mailed two months earlier. Hetty had sent it without knowing whether they were still living at the same address, nor whether they had even survived.

She wanted to get word to others to help her find Fritz as soon as she could. She had lost track of him for 15 months, which seemed like years, and they had promised each other to contact the Van Dykes first.

By the time they received her letters, it was July. Fritz had already been back in Amsterdam for several weeks, and after searching for her constantly without success or even a glimmer of hope, he had only just found her name on the list of survivors. They read Hetty's letter eagerly:

> *Dear Olivia, Sal, and Fleur,*
>
> *First of all, I want to let you know that I am still alive. After two years in concentration camps, we arrived in Sweden on May 4. I have*

gone through such an ordeal, you cannot imagine. I will tell you much more later on, but we were just told that for the time being we are staying in Sweden. The most important thing I need to know is about Fritz. Have you heard from him? He will certainly try to contact you. If he does write to you, please give him my address here, let him know that I am all right, that I am safe in Malmö. And let me know as fast as you can whether you have contacted him and if he is all right.

Being in Sweden is like being in a fairytale. We came by way of the Danish border, where we were handed over to the Swedish Red Cross by the SS officials – and it is unbelievable. This is such a relief, and I feel as if we are now in good hands, and everything will turn out all right. The people here are like angels, full of goodness. They laugh and are cheerful and they just want to make us happy. We are given the best food here, too, it's unreal! Everything here goes according to the doctor's orders. Dear ones, I am so full of stories, and I want to tell you everything. I will be writing often.

I understand that you have all gone through a lot in Holland, too. I have read all about it and never thought that you all would have to endure so much there also, but now let us look forward to the future. Please remember I have only one wish: That is to see Fritz again as soon as possible. I at least need to hear from him, because I have never lost faith that he is still alive. Please help me if you can, I am so grateful. I will stop now, and I send much love.

Wishing you all the best, Hetty

In the middle of July, Hetty received a telegram from Rosalie that Fritz was indeed alive and living at the Van Dyke's. The moment Hetty read the telegram, she was floating on air. Fritz was alive! She was alive in Sweden and Fritz was alive in Amsterdam, waiting for her. She immediately wrote a letter to Rosalie.

Dearest Rosalie and the rest of the family in America,

I am so ridiculously happy; I cannot tell you. I do not think there are words in any language to express how I feel. I had just finished sweeping the floors and was preparing to go downtown into Göteborg with a girlfriend this morning, when a woman supervisor came to our barracks with a piece of paper in her hand and said, "There is a telegram for you." I ran to her and quickly took it, expecting it was from you, but was not prepared for the news it brought. I very nearly pounced on her with glee, throwing my arms around her neck – Fritz is alive and well and at the Van Dykes!

All the women in our barracks screamed in excitement. There was such an eruption of cheer that my senses just shut down. It was so unbelievable that I just could not digest it and am near delirious. I am dizzy and my head is in the clouds. I cannot wait to travel to Holland. I am the second one here now who has heard that her husband is alive. Very few partners have surfaced of the women I know from the Philips group. Fritz never knew I had worked for Philips and never knew where to look for me.

Nearly all of my worries, fears, and doubts have been lifted from my shoulders. A weight has fallen from my heart.

I picture myself arriving by plane in Holland and Fritz will come to collect me. I think I am going to go crazy!

There may come a day when he and I can come together to New York. If you organize documents for Fritz, there must be an application form for couples, also, yes? Don't worry that you will be stuck caring for us, because Fritz is always able to earn a good living, and I want to tell you that when I came home yesterday, the money Uncle Daniel sent had arrived. I am so relieved, now I can buy some things we need to start over.

Everything is extremely expensive here, but you know I will buy only practical things. Who knows how long we will have to make do.

I do not want to change the mood of this letter by telling the story of the nine camps I was in. I will tell that story later. I have not yet received another letter from you, the post is just a mess. But please do keep writing, I am dying for news! Everyone talks about you as if you are my mother because you take such good care of me, and I am so proud. You are family!

Let me hear from you and give everyone my warmest greetings and many kisses from an ecstatic,

Hetty

37

JULY 1945

LETTERS BETWEEN HETTY AND FRITZ

When Fritz finally received the first letters from Hetty, the first two written in freedom, it was July 5, 1945. He began pouring out his heart to her, writing postcard after postcard and sending them to the address he had for the refugee camp in Sweden. It would take weeks before the postal service between Sweden and the Netherlands was again functional, but both Fritz and Hetty slowly began receiving the news they had longed for.

Dearest Fritz,

I am so insanely happy, I just do not have words for it. I cannot believe it is true that this much luck was waiting for me ... it's unbelievable. There comes a moment and the heavens open up.

Are you happy at Olivia's? I know you are in good hands, and that puts my mind at ease. Are you healthy? I was so worried and sad about you. Just when despair was at its worst and I was so unsure about everything, the wonderful message arrived that you were with Olivia and the girls. Aunt Rosalie telegrammed me. At night I lie awake, giggling in bed with joy. I try to be quiet, but I wake up the other girls.

I have received money from Rosalie and Daniel in New York and also mail from them, and they are all fine. I am planning to buy many beautiful things for you, and I haven't been sick, I feel just great. How are you? How do you look? I am writing fast and am in a hurry to see you. I am so crazy with happiness, I am going nuts. I hope to be in Holland soon; I will make sure I am with the first group going back if at all possible. Will you come get me from the airport? I have longed for you for such a long time, I am so glad I will be in your arms soon. Hours of hugs, always yours,

Hetty

Hetty Darling,

I think you understand how happy I was when finally, one day before your birthday, your letters of May 10 and May 13 arrived here. The best day of my life.

I had unwavering faith that I would get you back, because otherwise all the horror and suffering would have been for nothing. Even though we are married, I have to make a declaration of love to you – you are the only thing that matters to me. What you had to go through was unbelievably terrible. I always hoped that you women would not have to go through all that and thank goodness you made it. I too have endured and survived a lot, and after a thorough medical exam I have a clean bill of health.

Also, happy birthday and many more returns of the day to you, but never ever again without me! Darling, you cannot imagine how happy I was to receive your letter. I love you so much. I hope to be able to hug you very soon and I already kiss you endlessly in my thoughts,

Fritz

38

HETTY, JULY 1945

FACING THE FUTURE

Fritz and Hetty had each landed in different worlds at the end of the war, Hetty in a sort of wonderland and Fritz in a country needing repair. He would have to wait to see whether the Jews would be compensated for lost lives or property. Any compensation for stolen possessions, bank accounts, or valuables of any kind would become a paperwork nightmare – at best. Much time would be required filling in forms and engaging in a bureaucratic drama.

Would existing or new governing bodies help Dutch refugees and return everyone's rights? Or would they try to sidestep obligations for the Sinti, the Roma, the gays, the disabled, and the many other disenfranchised people, including the Jews?

In contrast, everything about Hetty's liberation in neutral Sweden was smooth. Refugees received enough fragrant soap, warm water, new clothing, good food, and hygienic care to finally feel free of filth – or close to free. Hetty repeatedly said she had longed for soap more than any other thing throughout her captivity. For her, hygiene was essential. She had always risen earlier than the other inmates in the camps in order to feel as clean as possible and to care for her body as best as she could.

Many Swedish families volunteered to help the camp survivors. Hetty spoke very highly of the Swedes in all her letters to loved ones and declared that they had restored her faith in human beings.

Uncle Daniel and Rosalie in New York had collected money from other relatives and wired it to her. Hetty was extremely grateful; it heartened her to realize that there were still people who were good and kind, and people she could rely on. Many other refugees were totally alone and abandoned, with no one to ask for aid.

Hetty wrote many letters to Olivia and her daughters inquiring about Fritz, asking what she should buy for him. *Has he got any of his clothing back? What does he need? What kind of shoes should I purchase?* Hetty was terribly eager to hear from him again, but their replies were slow. The postal delays were interminable.

Hetty's daily routine in Göteborg was filled with eating, meeting with officials, paperwork, waiting, trying (unsuccessfully) to relax, more eating, bits of sightseeing, cleaning, shopping, and writing letters. She was having fun, or trying to, but she was lonely and badly missing Fritz.

The first day they had arrived in Sweden after the war had ended, everything was taken from them and burned. Once showered and dressed in clean clothes, they were told to reassemble for a meal. The caregivers indicated that the women should walk over to the adjoining building, and they pointed them in the right direction. Hetty and the group of women walked to the building and entered the large dining room with beautifully set tables, all with linen, fine dinnerware, and silver-plated cutlery. Hetty and her group kept walking past the tables because they could not imagine that these tables had been set for them. They left the dining hall and walked farther in search of tables more in keeping with what might be more appropriate. They waited timidly in the hall, and when staff caught up with them, they asked why the women had not sat down in the dining room as instructed?

That is when Hetty realized that they had become accustomed to being treated like lesser humans. They had not only become used to horrific treatment in the camps, but they had come to not expect better, not even in Sweden. They did not believe that something beautiful could be waiting for them, or even that they could be expected to be treated well. They had internalized the racial discrimination and hatred intended to dehumanize them. What had they become? Hetty realized that they need to regain a sense of worthiness and think of themselves deserving the best that life can bring, not because of what they went through, but because every human being deserves that.

This one incident served as a lifelong reminder of how far the hatred had conditioned them. The Nazis had succeeded in breaking their will to the point that it could turn them into slaves and prisoners; but now, the women could begin to replenish their self-respect and would be proud citizens once again.

Hetty had no opportunities to telephone anyone in Holland; only postcards or a lightweight airmail letter were allowed. Even coupons to buy all kinds of items were rationed – but then it all changed. Finally, one day, letters began arriving regularly, and Hetty was practically overwhelmed with the many declarations of love and devotion from Fritz. His letters were loving and adoring, and she was filled with joy.

He had decided to forgive Elly and Niels Jansen for having abused the trust that was given them. He had gone back for dinner again and had moved into the two-room flat above their own apartment which they had offered him. Perhaps they felt guilty about how they had spent the money he had entrusted to them and the dresses of Hetty's that Elly had given away. It was a cozy place that he and Hetty could live in together and start over.

Aunt Rosalie and Richy wrote her long letters as well. Hetty began to feel like a little bit of normalcy had returned to life – she felt the love of family once again – a valuable thing that people do not adequately value until it is taken from them.

One day, marvelously, she was offered a place on a ship to Amsterdam – 30 days earlier than expected. She had already signed up to be one of the first to go home, but there were women who had children back in Holland who had priority for return. The Dutch merchant and cargo vessel, Bonaire, regularly transported freight and some passengers between Europe and the Dutch Antilles. The ship was set to sail from Sweden and had space for a few Dutch passengers. One woman, who had two children in hiding in the Netherlands, had refused to leave her gravely ill husband behind in Sweden, so Hetty was allowed to take her place.

The Bonaire would not sail straight for the Netherlands because the cargo on board had to be delivered elsewhere first. The vessel traveled via Ireland, Scotland, and England before reaching a Dutch harbor. The trip would take almost two weeks. Even so, Hetty was excited when they set sail from Sweden on July 29. She hastily telegrammed Fritz in the hope he would receive it in time to meet her at the dock where the Bonaire was scheduled to arrive, around August 12, three months after the war in Europe had ended.

Hetty was obsessed with seeing Fritz. The practical decisions that lay ahead took up most of her thinking time – thoughts about their future together, where to live, and when to have children. She had a lot on her mind as she sailed the waters of the North Sea.

Since she had been freed, there had not been a moment long enough for her to really process things or even catch her breath. Now, onboard ship, she would figure some things out. She was determined to look ahead and not look back on the six years of terror and two years of imprisonment she had endured. The complete isolation from everything and anything familiar had had a disabling effect on her self-esteem, and that recent incident in the Swedish dining hall illustrated this to her.

On board the ship, Hetty found it easier to push depressing thoughts away, but now and then horrifying images would intrude on her thoughts. It would take her decades before she unraveled the baggage of her past as a Nazi prisoner of war.

Thanks to her warm reception in Denmark and Sweden, Hetty was looking forward to Amsterdam; she was expecting the same warm welcome there. It did not occur to her that there may yet be lingering antisemitic sentiments.

When the war broke out, she was still living at home with her father and Hans. Now she was a grown, married woman and looked forward to running her own household. She had already purchased things for Fritz and for herself. She would have to borrow a sewing machine from Olivia to sew curtains and a bedspread. She would make their home so lovely that they would forget every ugly, filthy moment in those godforsaken barracks and the camps.

Fritz had written to her that they had an apartment above Niels and Elly Jansen to move into together. She was delighted daydreaming. She kept picturing what it would be like to look into the eyes of her husband again, and to reunite with Olivia and her daughters. She was going to help Fleur plan her wedding and meet Sally's new partner. She prayed Fritz was not disabled in any way. He would have told her if he was, wouldn't he?

She thought about people she had not yet found, hoping they would return soon. On board the Bonaire were two women who had not yet found their husbands, and grief lingered over them onboard. Hetty realized that she was one of the rare ones, and she had to be sensitive to the fate of the others. She might have many losses to grieve, but she was elated to have found Fritz. All the other relatives surely could not all be dead, could they?

Hetty had a new group of friends, all camp inmates from the Philips group, and most of them lived in Amsterdam. This is where the most support would come from, she was sure. But in the back of her mind something was nagging her, and she knew she could not dismiss the worries. The other women had similar concerns. They wondered whether they could ever feel at home in the Netherlands again.

39

FRITZ, AUGUST 1945

TRANSITION TO THE FUTURE

There is a period of time after a war ends in an occupied country that is uniquely positive. Fritz, like everyone else, felt free on many levels. There were no armed guards harassing people on street corners. Everyone felt free to walk around, day and night. The curfew was gone. Anyone and everyone could attend services or go to the cinema or to a concert. Everyone could use public transportation, own a house or go on vacation. People were not segregated anymore – and this alone was wonderfully reassuring.

Many people, like Fritz, were embracing a second life, starting out fresh, anticipating a purposeful and prosperous future, with equal rights for all. Fritz imagined a good life with Hetty and allowed himself to dream of opportunities yet to come. The Dutch population seemed relieved, too. Having their land occupied and all their movements monitored had affected everyone – especially in the cities. Because of the horrific discrimination incurred by the Nazis, the Dutch government decided to do away with class differences and to treat everyone as equals. However, this had a strange and adverse effect on the Jews.

For instance, the Jews had lost so much more than their synagogues, rights, and belongings. Instead of getting extra help in the midst of grieving the immense loss of life and possessions that no other group had suffered during the war, when they returned, they were refused extra assistance, treatment, and leniency. This treatment ended up putting the Jews at a disadvantage and worked adversely because they were now not eligible for exemption for back taxes incurred when they were expelled from the country and incarcerated by the enemy. Nor were they reimbursed for stolen bank accounts, deeds to property, or businesses. They were told that everyone had hardships and to go to the back of the line. Because of the lack of psychological insight and the cold attitude they encountered, the war only continued for them.

The Dutch were acting as though they had all resisted the invasion and that they had supported the Jews. Although that narrative suited them, this was not entirely the case. Although only a quarter of all Dutch citizens had supported the Nazis, they all felt victimized and had had little time or opportunity to help anyone else. They were preoccupied with their own lives and had no way of understanding what the camp trauma had done to the survivors. Even those who tried comprehending were not able to understand what the victims had had to endure.

Although persecution can be explained, it cannot be felt. They all needed extra care; no one really knew how to help them or even where to begin. In 1945, there were no psychologists trained to guide people through trauma. Parents returning often had trouble finding their children because the addresses of hosting families had been lost, many had left the country, and others had just disappeared. Some survivors never found their children. Some were refused their children because people worried that they were not capable of raising children properly and, after all, the children now had new identities and had become Christian, for instance.

Hundreds of children did return from concentration camps – but without adults; they came by train after the liberation, but many were so young that they never knew their family names, and thus were never able to be reunited with relatives. Workers in the Resistance did not, of course, share information about real names and hiding places. Some older children had also moved around a lot from one hosting family to another, which made tracking them difficult, time-consuming, and often impossible. Advertisements searching for people ran in the newspapers; ads that would periodically appear for decades to come. Some who were babies or young children when the war began did not recognize their birth parents after five years and resisted leaving their host families because their biological parents had become complete strangers to them.

The company of family and friends was paramount in re-establishing communities; yet, in some cities, synagogues remained empty because the entire congregation had been wiped out. It was a time when the Jews tried to resume the old way of life, but with many lone parents and orphaned children, they became desperately unhappy, lost, and alone.

Dinners with Elly and Niels Jansen had prepared Fritz for some hard realities he had not yet faced. His leisurely dinners with them had revealed that this seemingly nice couple were living in a parallel universe. Both seemed naïve, and above all, uninterested. They were practically indifferent to those who were still trapped in the middle of tragedy. They pretended that there was only rejoicing to do. Elly and Niels thought that offering Fritz and Hetty shelter in the apartment upstairs was a generous offer. After learning that they had spent all the money that Fritz had entrusted to them, he thought it was the least they could do. They had also said they had given away Hetty's clothing – her own designs – because they did not expect her to return.

The country needed mending. The government needed to find its way. The Dutch had reclaimed their land from the Germans and had dealt with the traitors and collaborators who had helped eliminate so many Jews. But that nagging feeling would not go away and solidified when no real justice was achieved, and the perpetrators were not severely punished. Even the Nazis and collaborators who went on trial received three good meals a day and comfortable prison cells, never knowing or acknowledging their crimes nor showing any remorse. Some would justify their heinous deeds until their dying day.

While Fritz was regaining his sense of freedom after years of feeling hunted, he still had mountains of pain to sort through. He realized that Niels and Elly had no idea at all what it was like for those who were taken captive and brutally tortured – they simply could not comprehend the horrors. They had never even thought about what months of starvation could do to the minds and souls of famished people. When these difficult subjects edged into conversations, Fritz was more than a little disappointed with their complete lack of empathy. He did not believe that the Jansens' idea of friendship and trust mirrored his.

"No one will ever understand what we went through unless they go through the same thing themselves," Fritz quietly told them one evening. It was the beginning of a new understanding for Fritz because, like the appeal of motion pictures, the viewer is given an opportunity to experience some of the difficult themes in life without going through the actual experience itself. That is what a good book offers, he concluded, because in fact, it could be considered desirable to understand imprisonment without ever having to become a captive, Fritz thought.

Instead of attempting to convince his hosts of the truth, because he realized they just weren't capable of understanding, he just smiled and allowed them their own interpretation and memories of the war.

"Looking back at when we had to register as Jews in early 1941," Fritz said, "I am sad that we all obeyed. We might not have gone along with the Nazis' demands if we had known that the Jewish council had been cooperating with them or what the outcome could possible entail."

But Elly and Niels did not seem interested enough to listen to Fritz's thoughts. He decided that, should some similar threat ever arise during his lifetime, he would immediately gather his family together and emigrate with Hetty to a free country. From day one of being freed, Fritz had kept this in mind and would soon start planning an exit from Europe. He decided he wanted to always be prepared for oppression. After reclaiming his rights, he would acquire the paperwork necessary for his family to be ready to leave at a moment's notice.

Ultimately, the friendship with the Jansens would end when Elly showed up for dinner months later wearing Hetty's clothing. She had apparently forgotten where the dress had come from and seemed totally insensitive to her own behavior and what it meant for Fritz and Hetty.

The war ended even worse, though, for the perpetrators. All of Germany suffered the same humiliation at the end of World War II as they had experienced following the first World War. They had fallen from grace. Their fascist leader, Hitler, and his generals had abandoned their countrymen and had taken the cowardly way out. Instead of facing consequences and showing bravery, they committed suicide or fled to other countries, leaving most of their country in ruins, in a state of chaos, letting others pay for their crimes. Dr. Mengele escaped to South America after the war and evaded justice for his crimes, dying in Brazil in 1979.

40

FRITZ & HETTY, AUGUST 1945

THE RENDEZVOUS

As Hetty's ship approached, the land seemed to grow larger in her eyes. Her heart was swelling with longing. Only a few people were waiting on the dock; she was, after all, on a cargo ship. Only eight Dutch passengers from the Swedish refugee camp were aboard. In the distance, Hetty could see the dark hair on the back of a man's head, and she was quite sure she recognized Fritz's posture. He was holding flowers and talking to someone. Then he turned his head toward the ship, and Hetty could see Fritz's eyes searching for her. In the next moment, their eyes met.

He looked exactly as he had the first time she ever lay eyes on him from the bay window of her family's flat when she was reading and he was gazing up at her; only he looked wiser and more capable. Her hands gripped the railing, and a slight feeling of nausea and lightheadedness took her breath away. Why would she be nervous about seeing Fritz? She stood alone in the wind smiling brightly down at him. At the same time, tears rolled down her cheeks as his expression deepened and his big brown eyes glowed. She began sobbing and gasped, her fingers covering her mouth as she wept. Fritz shook his head in amazement and a crooked smile appeared on his face. His Hetty was back.

The rope opened to let passengers through, and Hetty disembarked gleefully, descending the gangplank, and walking toward him carrying her belongings in both hands. Her surroundings all but faded as she approached Fritz. He could not get past the ropes on his end, and he waited impatiently.

She picked up her pace, moving faster, then dropped both bags to run to him. He knew exactly how to capture her in his arms, lifting and twirling her around, before lowering her feet once more to the ground. He had nearly forgotten how tiny she was, but she looked well. She had nearly forgotten how much taller he was. He seemed different somehow, stronger. They knew that a new life together had begun. It was the beginning of something they both had longed for and had visualized since they were separated in March 1944.

Fritz reached into his pocket and pulled out something wrapped in silk to give to her. He wrapped her fingers around the tiny package. His eyes were mischievous, and he told her, "We are already married, so do not expect this to be an engagement ring. I promised to keep an image of you in my mind, in our Memory Place," he said, "and you made that possible. I was able to go on, to survive, because of your beautiful smile and the hope of seeing you again and taking you in my arms. That moment is here. Our Memory Place served us well."

"I have wanted to tell you something since the day I disappeared out of your life," he stated. "Remember, I was about to board the train, and I could not say goodbye to you. There were so many of us leaving our wives behind. I was so afraid for you. I was worried you would feel lost and abandoned and that you might lose all hope. I wanted to forge an important message in your mind that my love would envelop you always, and that my love would never abandon you or judge you for what you may have to do to stay alive. I was crying, standing in line, picturing your forgiving, kind, and loving nature and fortifying it with hope and love. I stood sending you strength and the will to live, vowing to be your devoted husband until death do us part and beyond. Especially because I couldn't see you anywhere and we couldn't even wave goodbye, I just kept sending you my heartfelt intentions. A moment later, something amazing happened."

"Someone pressed something into my hand, and I sensed that I shouldn't look at the bearer of this small keepsake I was given, but I couldn't help it. I recognized Hunchy as he marched away from me with his face down, his back toward me, careful not to acknowledge me. I had no idea what he had put into my hand. I had to wait until no guards were watching before I looked to see what he had handed me. It was a sign, an answer from you that you had heard me and we would survive."

Hetty knew what it was. She squeezed his hand, holding hers. She unfolded the silk square to find the tiny passport photo that she had asked Hunchy to give Fritz – something she'd nearly forgotten about.

"When Hunchy brought me this I knew it would carry me through," Fritz said. "Whenever I could, I took out the photo in the dark in my bunk. It is tattered now, but it made it through everything, just like I did." Fritz kissed Hetty long and hard and whispered into her ear something that made her toes curl. She was standing on her tiptoes and looked around a bit nervously. She smiled and felt woozy inside. Fritz said something quite inappropriate for polite company, and she was blushing. As they walked away from the ship, the whisper resonated between them, having something to do with being so happy to be alive, happy for so much, but mostly for being back together and being more than ready to start working on their future family.

Fritz and Hetty after the war ended in 1945 on the day she hears she is expecting their first child.

The official farewell picture for the Dutch friends and family before departing for America in 1951

EPILOGUE

Hetty would later learn that her entire Dutch family in the Netherlands had been wiped out, and that she was the only survivor. She had great difficulty accepting that so many relatives were just gone. For a long time, her eyes would scan crowds, looking for them. She spent her remaining years thinking of her brother and her father daily.

Fritz and Hetty were happy together in Amsterdam after the war. They had two daughters, whom they loved very much. They then immigrated to the United States in April 1951. The family made its way west from New York to California, with a few lengthy stops along the way. Lisabelle and Lena both survived, but their entire family, including Lena's husband and his family, perished. Together, mother and daughter came to visit Hetty and Fritz in New York City. There, Lisabelle ended up marrying Fritz's cousin, Henry (who had lived in the attic with his parents for so long during the war), and settled down. It would take Lisabelle years to overcome the nightmares, achieving that by speaking about her experiences at schools in New York City. Dottie and Hetty would drift apart and lose track of one another until, one day in California, they happened upon each other because their daughters had become best friends in grade school.

The family would all become naturalized American citizens five years later and would encounter new challenges as they moved around, restless, and searching for safety. Eventually, Fritz, Hetty, and the girls would assimilate and settle in the San Francisco Bay area. Dottie's sister Iris, the translator at Bergen-Belsen, also survived and settled in Southern California.

"I did not believe in a God until I had rescued myself at Auschwitz," Hetty said much later, "because the miracle of surviving Auschwitz could only be attributed to a higher force."

The American customs and culture took some getting used to. Learning what was expected of them was an ongoing process. Fritz and Hetty had to decide whom they could trust. Trust issues turned out to be a problem for the children, too. Their parents would tell them, "Don't talk about our background. Don't mention that we are Jewish or were in Nazi concentration camps." The children were raised to keep other secrets, too, without ever understanding why, which caused misplaced shame they carried around with them. Hetty had separation anxiety, fearful that each goodbye could be the last. Their children would constantly try not to disappoint, somehow feeling like they had to replace the Jews who had been killed or lost. Hetty's paranoia increased with age, and she frequently had conflicts with others.

Second-generation children of war victims learn many adult skills at a young age. Both of Fritz and Hetty's daughters grew up doubting themselves because of moving around so much. They made no lasting friendships. They knew how to protect their parents on a daily basis; yet, they did not have their own needs met in the process. It was as though they were the parents. This becomes a problem because it blurs the boundaries between the roles. Each generation born after a war or a family trauma inherits the pain that shows up in their lives, but in different ways. The pain and loss occupy a large place in the homes of war victims, in their children and grandchildren, and in those who fought in those wars.

Fritz, too, was the only one of his Jewish family to survive World War II. He thought he could keep the tragic years in the past, far from his children's lives; but in reality, nothing could. Their children, as adults, were able to ultimately unravel the problems they had inherited from their traumatized parents; however, it took time before the medical community, in general, would understand that trauma is passed down generationally and genetically. Based in part on what had happened to the victims of World War II, scientists learned that trauma is visible in the DNA of the victims' offspring, referred to as epigenetics. It would take even more years for the second and later generations to identify and try to understand its effects. If people avoid talking about trauma, it is not processed and is instead transferred down the generational chain in disturbing ways.

After only nine years in America, Fritz developed a serious illness as a result of war-related trauma when his limbs had frozen after jumping off a train and walking for hours in frozen snow. He died on January 1, 1960, after a year of hospitalization, at only 54 years old. Hetty found herself a widow at age 39, grief stricken again; her girls aged only nine and 13. A few years after Fritz died, Hetty became a custom knitwear designer and created popular clothing designs that would never go out of fashion, earning enough to provide well for her family. Later, she survived two bouts of cancer and another immigration, this time back to Amsterdam, after having lived in America for 40 years. Despite many hardships, Hetty's resilience was remarkable.

The children always admired and adored their parents. Their father was a true gentleman, old-school style. Hetty's strength, determination, and lust for life were especially impressive. She had an eye for beauty and created many gorgeous things throughout her lifetime. Hetty was always impeccably dressed, and she never drank alcohol or took drugs. She had always emphasized the importance of education and self-reliance. She was adamant that her children grow up to be self-sufficient adults, and both graduated from American universities. They were successful in their professions as well as in their relationships, and both daughters are today staunch advocates of respecting human rights.

Unfortunately, Hetty's suffering never ended, and she developed an illness called "persecution complex," suspecting even good-intentioned folks to ridicule and stalk her. "You can take the person out of the war, but you can't take the war out of the person," tells her story. Her daughters spent the last 40 years of her life rescuing her from her fears and battling with her over trust issues. Hetty lived to be 95, and she maintained her sense of humor throughout her life. She was terribly bright, never missed the news, and knew the names of all the US government officials. She was well-informed, voting in every election, right until the end. She led a life of decency and dignity and was always sympathetic to the underdogs of society. She deserves respect and admiration for a long life of dedication to fighting against the injustices of the world.

Their eldest daughter went into politics and was able to fight for justice by designing new laws introducing equality measures and running American government agencies. Their youngest daughter, a visual artist, made a three-part artistic monument dedicated to the postwar generations. It is composed of a 40-year-long oeuvre of paintings that tell their own stories, an installation with 105 portraits, diaries, and film interviews, among others, with Eva Schloss, Anne Frank's posthumous stepsister. This book completes the trilogy.

HISTORICAL TIMELINE

11 September 1939 Germany invades Poland and declares war.

10 May 1940 Germany declares war on The Netherlands. After five days of bombing Rotterdam, The Netherlands capitulates.

January 1941 All Dutch Jews forced to register and subsequently lose their citizenship and all their rights.

7 December 1941 Japan bombs Pearl Harbor (in Hawaii) involving the USA.

30 March 1942 Brother Hans summoned to appear at Nazi headquarters and leaves Amsterdam.

1 May 1942 Jews must wear a star of David on all clothes in and outside of the home.

18 May 1942 Hetty and Fritz first meet.

16 July 1942 Resistance Meeting with first rumors of extermination camps.

17 July 1942 Hetty and Fritz marry in secret.

11 September 1942 Martin Golden vanishes.

14 January 1943 Hetty and Fritz are summoned by Nazis to appear in Nazi headquarters where their papers are reviewed, but are surprisingly free to go after 48 hours.

17 January 1943 a 'Sperr' is stamped in Hetty's and Fritz's passports and they are free to go.

8 June 1943 Hetty and Fritz are arrested from their apartment in Amsterdam as they sleep, and deported 72 hours later.

11 June 1943 Hetty and Fritz arrive in Camp Vught.

20 March 1944 Fritz and other men are evacuated from Camp Vught and Hetty and Fritz are split up.

Fritz:

Fritz goes to Camp Westerbork, and was later transferred to another train.

Fritz goes to Auschwitz.

Fritz Auschwitz Monowitz .

Fritz Auschwitz Birkenau.

Fritz goes to Buna.

Fritz to Landskrone Prison.

Fritz goes to Brünnlitz.

Hetty:

20 March 1944 Fritz and men leave Camp Vught.

3 June 1944 Philips Women evacuated from Camp Vught.

6 June 1944 D-Day in Normandy, France. Allied Forces land.

6 June 1944 Hetty and 400 women and 100 men from Philips Group arrived in Auschwitz.

13 June 1944 Hetty and the remaining 250 from Philips Group went to Reichenbach (Underground in the mountain).

20 January 1945 Hetty and remaining Philips Group women put on transport to Sportschule, Langenbielau 1 (for 4 weeks) (Spinning mill).

18 February 1945 Death March. Hetty and Philips Group on transport to Trautenau (Czechoslovakia).

3 March 1945 Hetty and Philips group to Porta Westfalica to work deep underground until April 1, 1945 (4 weeks) (Northern Germany).

1 April 1945 Hetty and what is left of the Philips Group put on transport to Beendorf, Braunsweig (Northern Germany).

10 April 1945 on transport for three weeks, destination unknown. Train goes back and forth without food. Women crushed into cattle cars with 140 women. Hamburg.

20 April 1945 train stops in Bergen-Belsen concentration camp. It is full and they cannot disembark the train.

20 April 1945 Hetty and group go on another Death March over mountain ranges.

30 April 1945 Hitler, Göhring and both families and others commit suicide.

1 May 1945 Philips Group are clubbed out of train and board a train with straw on the ground which must mean something good. Many die of total exhaustion, starvation and typhoid fever en route.

2 May 1945 Hetty and Philips Group arrive in a small camp in Eidelstedt, Germany. They arrive after 10 days of no food in impoverished condition.

2 May 1945 Hetty and Philips Group are freed at the border between Germany and Denmark. The remaining group go by boat to a refugee camp for Dutch groups in Malmö, Sweden.

4 May 1945 Hetty and Philips Group go to Gothenburg.

5 May 1945 War declared officially over in The Netherlands.

8 May 1945 War declared officially over in Europe.

10 May 1945 Hetty announces her survival to the Van Dykes in Amsterdam, but due to postal delays all the letters cross each other and arrive in June and in a different sequence than they were written.

12 August 1945 Hetty goes by boat from Sweden to Amsterdam

14 August 1945 Japan officially surrenders after two U.S. atomic bombings in Hiroshima and Nagasaki.

Hans Golden:

2 October 1942 Hetty's Brother Hans deported to an extermination camp from a slave labor camp – never to return.

31 August 1943 Hans dies somewhere in mid-Europe.

Martin Golden:

11 September 1942 Martin deported and killed one week later in Sobibor or Auschwitz.

SUPPLEMENTAL READING

https://www.jpost.com/christian-news/the-dutch-electronics-company-exec-who-helped-save-more-than-300-jews-in-wwii-474474

https://encyclopedia.ushmm.org/content/en/article/oskar-schindler

https://khc.qcc.cuny.edu/camps/text/

https://encyclopedia.ushmm.org/content/en/article/einsatzgruppen

https://encyclopedia.ushmm.org/content/en/article/nazi-medical-experiments?parent=en%2F135

List of major concentration camps: jewishvirtuallibrary.org/list-of-major-nazi-concentration-camps

https://encyclopedia.ushmm.org/content/en/article/final-solution-in-depth

The killing nurses of the Third Reich: youtube.com/watch?v=Rz8ge4aw8Ws hmd.org.uk/resource/14-july-1933-sterilisation-of-germans-with-disabilities/

britannica.com/topic/Hitler-Youth

timeline.com/the-nazi-breeding-and-infanticide-program-you-probably-never-knew-about-cc5cc7b82fdc

amazon.com/Spear-Destiny-Occult-Behind-pierced/dp/0877285470 This book explains Hitler's involvement with the Occult.

Taken from the film *Where the Holocaust Began* from the Imperial War Museum, England on BBC Two.

See Kristallnacht, the night of broken glass,

https://www.latimes.com/archives/la-xpm-2002-dec-01-adfg-bountyhunt1-story.html

The Final Solution was Hitler's official plan of genocide to wipe out Jews and other undesirables.

encyclopedia.ushmm.org/content/en/article/final-solution-in-depth

en.wikipedia.org/wiki/Final_Solution

historiek.net/arierverklaring-voor-nederlandse-ambtenaren-1940/137680/

Listings of all restrictions against the Dutch Jewish community in World War II. https://www.tracesofwar.com/articles/2659/Anti-Jewish-measures-in-the-Netherlands-since-1940.htm

encyclopedia.ushmm.org/content/en/timeline-event/holocaust/1939-1941/jewish-badge-decreed

https://encyclopedia.ushmm.org/content/en/article/josef-mengele

Bales of haircloth and almost two tons of hair belonging to almost 40,000 people can be seen at the Auschwitz Memorial. https://www.

yadvashem.org/yv/en/exhibitions/women-in-the-holocaust/womanhood/hair.asp

almanac.com/fact/whatever-happened-to-the-12-tribes-of#:~:text=The%20tribes%20were%20named%20after,of%20Judah%20and%20Benjamin%20survived.

history.com/topics/world-war-ii/d-day

https://www.sobibor.org/en/4-what-is-meant-by-the-children-transports/

britannica.com/topic/SS

https://encyclopedia.ushmm.org/search?query=classification+system&languages%5B%5D=en

https://www.jewishvirtuallibrary.org/site-search?q=kapos

The Main Administrative Nazi headquarters was located on Gerrit van der Veenstraat 99 in Amsterdam.

https://jck.nl/en/location/hollandsche-schouwburg

https://encyclopedia.ushmm.org/content/en/article/german-police-in-the-nazi-state

https://encyclopedia.ushmm.org/content/en/article/gestapo

https://auschwitz.camp/en/traces/buna-factory-in-monowitz/

https://www.imdb.com/title/tt6600720/ "Hitler's Circle of Evil," a Netflix series, has 10 episodes and describes in detail the role of each deputy and how they influenced and competed with each other.

https://oaktrust.library.tamu.edu/items/4b485dcd-cf77-4418-b559-a4aa3c47f86a

The later-estimated value of the property stolen from the Jews would amount to billions in stolen wealth. The 2014 film *Monuments Men* was based on a 2007 non-fiction book by Robert M. Edsel and Bret

Witter; it follows a group of Allied officers tasked with finding and saving pieces of art and other culturally important items before Nazis destroyed or stole them during World War II. According to George Clooney, "Eighty percent of the story is still completely true and accurate, and almost all of the scenes happened."

https://www.joodsmonument.nl/en/page/740137/sportschule-langenbielau-reichenbach

encyclopedia.ushmm.org/content/en/article/the-murder-of-people-with-disabilities

https://www.theguardian.com/world/2019/jan/25/nazi-north-american-holocaust-book-canada-national-archive

See real footage from the Frontline documentary, *Memory of the Camps*, which had been directed in part by Alfred Hitchcock in 1945. This film was shelved for 30 years following WWII and was resurrected by PBS in 1985. It is **not** for children's viewing. https://www.pbs.org/wgbh/frontline/documentary/memory-of-the-camps/

https://psycom.net/trauma/epigenetics-trauma

After gaining 16 kilos in 8 weeks, Hetty (second from left) is happy with her campmates on board the vessel Bonaire on her way home to Amsterdam to meet Fritz

ABOUT THE AUTHOR

Monica van Rijn is a multi-disciplinary, internationally known visual artist with more than 200 exhibitions to her name. Born in the Netherlands in 1950, the child of two Holocaust survivors, Monica grew up in California, where she studied art, sociology, and philosophy. Her poetry evolved into songwriting while she traveled for a year on her own, after which she settled in Amsterdam. There, she attended painting and writing classes for five years.

She interviewed her mother on a regular basis, building a large, interactive "monument of stories" called *Colored by War*, which she dedicated to all generations impacted by war. She then began guest speaking and writing her parents' memoir. Through her compelling storytelling, she describes how it was possible to survive so many concentration camps and labor camps. Monica is an inspiring guest speaker who captures the attention of audiences across the globe.

Visit her website at www.monicavanrijn.com.

AMSTERDAM PUBLISHERS
HOLOCAUST LIBRARY

The series **Holocaust Survivor Memoirs World War II** consists of the following autobiographies of survivors:

The Dead Years. Holocaust Memoirs, by Joseph Schupack

Hank Brodt Holocaust Memoirs. A Candle and a Promise, by Deborah Donnelly

Rescued from the Ashes. The Diary of Leokadia Schmidt, Survivor of the Warsaw Ghetto, by Leokadia Schmidt

My Lvov. Holocaust Memoir of a twelve-year-old Girl, by Janina Hescheles

Remembering Ravensbrück. From Holocaust to Healing, by Natalie Hess

Wolf. A Story of Hate, by Zeev Scheinwald with Ella Scheinwald

Save my Children. An Astonishing Tale of Survival and its Unlikely Hero, by Leon Kleiner with Edwin Stepp

Holocaust Memoirs of a Bergen-Belsen Survivor & Classmate of Anne Frank, by Nanette Blitz Konig

Defiant German - Defiant Jew. A Holocaust Memoir from inside the Third Reich, by Walter Leopold with Les Leopold

In a Land of Forest and Darkness. The Holocaust Story of two Jewish Partisans, by Sara Lustigman Omelinski

Holocaust Memories. Annihilation and Survival in Slovakia, by Paul Davidovits

From Auschwitz with Love. The Inspiring Memoir of Two Sisters' Survival, Devotion and Triumph Told by Manci Grunberger Beran & Ruth Grunberger Mermelstein, by Daniel Seymour

Remetz. Resistance Fighter and Survivor of the Warsaw Ghetto, by Jan Yohay Remetz

My March Through Hell. A Young Girl's Terrifying Journey to Survival, by Halina Kleiner with Edwin Stepp

Roman's Journey, by Roman Halter

Beyond Borders. Escaping the Holocaust and Fighting the Nazis. 1938-1948, by Rudi Haymann

The Engineers. A memoir of survival through World War II in Poland and Hungary, by Henry Reiss

Spark of Hope. An Autobiography, by Luba Wrobel Goldberg

Footnote to History. From Hungary to America. The Memoir of a Holocaust Survivor, by Andrew Laszlo

Farewell Atlantis. Recollections, by Valentīna Freimane

The Courtyard. A memoir, by Benjamin Parket and Alexa Morris

The Mulberry Tree. The story of a life before and after the Holocaust, by Iboja Wandall-Holm

The Boy in the Back. A True Story of Survival in Auschwitz and Mauthausen, as told to Fern Lebo by Jan Blumenstein

Beneath the Lightless Sky. Surviving the Holocaust in the Sewers of Lvov, by Ignacy Chiger

From Sorrow to Joy. From Hitler's Darkness to the Sunlight on Mount Carmel, by Dr. Yakov Adler

Mendel Run, by Milton H. Schwartz

The Kapos of Auschwitz, by Charles Liblau

The series **Holocaust Survivor True Stories**
consists of the following biographies:

Among the Reeds. The true story of how a family survived the Holocaust, by Tammy Bottner

A Holocaust Memoir of Love & Resilience. Mama's Survival from Lithuania to America, by Ettie Zilber

Living among the Dead. My Grandmother's Holocaust Survival Story of Love and Strength, by Adena Bernstein Astrowsky

Heart Songs. A Holocaust Memoir, by Barbara Gilford

Shoes of the Shoah. The Tomorrow of Yesterday, by Dorothy Pierce

Hidden in Berlin. A Holocaust Memoir, by Evelyn Joseph Grossman

Separated Together. The Incredible True WWII Story of Soulmates Stranded an Ocean Apart, by Kenneth P. Price, Ph.D.

The Man Across the River. The incredible story of one man's will to survive the Holocaust, by Zvi Wiesenfeld

If Anyone Calls, Tell Them I Died. A Memoir, by Emanuel (Manu) Rosen

The House on Thrömerstrasse. A Story of Rebirth and Renewal in the Wake of the Holocaust, by Ron Vincent

Dancing with my Father. His hidden past. Her quest for truth. How Nazi Vienna shaped a family's identity, by Jo Sorochinsky

The Story Keeper. Weaving the Threads of Time and Memory - A Memoir, by Fred Feldman

Krisia's Silence. The Girl who was not on Schindler's List, by Ronny Hein

Defying Death on the Danube. A Holocaust Survival Story, by Debbie J. Callahan with Henry Stern

A Doorway to Heroism. A decorated German-Jewish Soldier who became an American Hero, by W. Jack Romberg

The Shoemaker's Son. The Life of a Holocaust Resister, by Laura Beth Bakst

The Redhead of Auschwitz. A True Story, by Nechama Birnbaum

Land of Many Bridges. My Father's Story, by Bela Ruth Samuel Tenenholtz

Creating Beauty from the Abyss. The Amazing Story of Sam Herciger, Auschwitz Survivor and Artist, by Lesley Ann Richardson

On Sunny Days We Sang. A Holocaust Story of Survival and Resilience, by Jeannette Grunhaus de Gelman

Painful Joy. A Holocaust Family Memoir, by Max J. Friedman

I Give You My Heart. A True Story of Courage and Survival, by Wendy Holden

In the Time of Madmen, by Mark A. Prelas

Monsters and Miracles. Horror, Heroes and the Holocaust, by Ira Wesley Kitmacher

Flower of Vlora. Growing up Jewish in Communist Albania, by Anna Kohen

Aftermath: Coming of Age on Three Continents. A Memoir, by Annette Libeskind Berkovits

Not a real Enemy. The True Story of a Hungarian Jewish Man's Fight for Freedom, by Robert Wolf

Zaidy's War. Four Armies, Three Continents, Two Brothers. One Man's Impossible Story of Endurance, by Martin Bodek

The Glassmaker's Son. Looking for the World my Father left behind in Nazi Germany, by Peter Kupfer

The Apprentice of Buchenwald. The True Story of the Teenage Boy Who Sabotaged Hitler's War Machine, by Oren Schneider

Good for a Single Journey, by Helen Joyce

Burying the Ghosts. She escaped Nazi Germany only to have her life torn apart by the woman she saved from the camps: her mother, by Sonia Case

American Wolf. From Nazi Refugee to American Spy. A True Story, by Audrey Birnbaum

Bipolar Refugee. A Saga of Survival and Resilience, by Peter Wiesner

In the Wake of Madness. My Family's Escape from the Nazis, by Bettie Lennett Denny

Before the Beginning and After the End, by Hymie Anisman

I Will Give Them an Everlasting Name. Jacksonville's Stories of the Holocaust, by Samuel Cox

Hiding in Holland. A Resistance Memoir, by Shulamit Reinharz

The Ghosts on the Wall. A Grandson's Memoir of the Holocaust, by Kenneth D. Wald

Thirteen in Auschwitz. My grandmother's fight to stay human, by Lauren Meyerowitz Port

The Jewish Woman Who Fought the Nazis. Bep Schaap-Bedak's life during the Holocaust in Holland, by Eli Schaap

Little Edna's War. A True story of Resistance and Hope. A Gripping WWII page-turner, by Janet Bond Brill, PhD

Voices of Resilience. An Anthology of Stories written by Children of Holocaust Survivors, Edited by Deborah (Devora) Ross-Grayman

Was it just a matter of luck? A Family, the Holocaust, and the Founding of a Museum, by Dr Charles Kaner

Dreaming of the River. A Mother and Daughter's Fight for Survival during the Holocaust, by Pauline Steinhorn

From One Generation to the Next. Unbroken Resilience, by Hymie Anisman

The World has Caught Fire, by Leah Grisham PhD

The series **Jewish Children in the Holocaust** consists of the following autobiographies of Jewish children hidden during WWII in the Netherlands:

Searching for Home. The Impact of WWII on a Hidden Child, by Joseph Gosler

Sounds from Silence. Reflections of a Child Holocaust Survivor, Psychiatrist and Teacher, by Robert Krell

Sabine's Odyssey. A Hidden Child and her Dutch Rescuers, by Agnes Schipper

The Journey of a Hidden Child, by Harry Pila and Robin Black

Out of the Woods, by Aliza Levy Erber

The series **New Jewish Fiction** consists of the following novels, written by Jewish authors. All novels are set in the time during or after the Holocaust.

The Corset Maker. A Novel, by Annette Libeskind Berkovits

Escaping the Whale. The Holocaust is over. But is it ever over for the next generation? by Ruth Rotkowitz

When the Music Stopped. Willy Rosen's Holocaust, by Casey Hayes

Hands of Gold. One Man's Quest to Find the Silver Lining in Misfortune, by Roni Robbins

The Girl Who Counted Numbers. A Novel, by Roslyn Bernstein

There was a garden in Nuremberg. A Novel, by Navina Michal Clemerson

The Butterfly and the Axe, by Omer Bartov

To Live Another Day. A Novel, by Elizabeth Rosenberg

The Right to Happiness. After all they went through. Stories, by Helen Schary Motro

Five Amber Beads, by Richard Aronowitz

To Love Another Day. A Novel, by Elizabeth Rosenberg

Cursing the Darkness. A Novel about Loss and Recovery, by Joanna Rosenthall

The series **Holocaust Heritage** consists of the following memoirs by 2G:

The Cello Still Sings. A Generational Story of the Holocaust and of the Transformative Power of Music, by Janet Horvath

The Fire and the Bonfire. A Journey into Memory, by Ardyn Halter

The Silk Factory: Finding Threads of My Family's True Holocaust Story, by Michael Hickins

Winter Light. The Memoir of a Child of Holocaust Survivors, by Grace Feuerverger

Out from the Shadows. Growing up with Holocaust Survivor Parents, by Willie Handler

Hidden in Plain Sight. A Family Memoir and the Untold Story of the Holocaust in Serbia, by Julie Brill

The Unspeakable. Breaking my family's silence surrounding the Holocaust, by Nicola Hanefeld

Eighteen for Life. Surviving the Holocaust,

by Helen Schamroth

Four Survivor Grandparents. Run. Rely. Rebuild, by Jonathan Schloss

Austrian Again. Reclaiming a Lost Legacy,

by Anne Hand

Never Fitting In. My Journey with Parental Trauma, Addiction, Healing, by Sonia Claire Ascher

Divine Corners. In the Shadow of the Holocaust on a Catskills Chicken Farm, by Michelle Friedman

Milk in an Eggshell. Living with a Family's Open Secrets, by Miryam Sas

The series **Holocaust Books for Young Adults** consists of the following novels, based on true stories:

The Boy behind the Door. How Salomon Kool Escaped the Nazis. Inspired by a True Story, by David Tabatsky

Running for Shelter. A True Story, by Suzette Sheft

The Precious Few. An Inspirational Saga of Courage based on True Stories, by David Twain with Art Twain

Dark Shadows Hover, by Jordan Steven Sher

The Sun will Shine Again, by Cynthia Goldstein Monsour

The Memory Place. How My Parents Survived Nazi Hell, by Monica van Rijn

The series **WWII Historical Fiction** consists of the following novels, some of which are based on true stories:

Mendelevski's Box. A Heartwarming and Heartbreaking Jewish Survivor's Story, by Roger Swindells

Brave Face. The Inspiring WWII Memoir of a Dutch/German Child, by I. Caroline Crocker and Meta A. Evenbly

When We Had Wings. The Gripping Story of an Orphan in Janusz Korczak's Orphanage. A Historical Novel, by Tami Shem-Tov

Jacob's Courage. Romance and Survival amidst the Horrors of War, by Charles S. Weinblatt

A Semblance of Justice. Based on true Holocaust experiences, by Wolf Holles

Under the Pink Triangle. Where forbidden love meets unspeakable evil, by Katie Moore

www.ingramcontent.com/pod-product-compliance
Ingram Content Group UK Ltd.
Pitfield, Milton Keynes, MK11 3LW, UK
UKHW042207240426
12086UKWH00002B/325

9 789493 418547